Philadelphians

Philadelphians

Tony DePaul

Art by Jared Owens

NewPlainsPress.com

Author: Tony DePaul 1944-

First Printing, 2021. Printed in the United States of America.

Published by Agreement by Summerfield Publishing d.b.a. New Plains Press, PO Box 1946, Auburn, AL 36831-1946.

Email: publisher@newplainspress.com

ISBN 13: 978-1-7345719-8-1

CONTENTS

Introduction

The Philadelphians are here. Young, old, rich, poor, all races, creeds and gender. They thrive on the DNA of a three-hundred-and-thirty-year-old City that is at once Historical and hip, rundown and built up, peaceful and violent, growing and dying. The hopes, fears, dreams and regrets of the Philadelphians reverberate in their stories like blood charging through veins. Their tales are unique and ubiquitous. They are separate people and all people. They are you and me. Jump aboard the Septa train or bus or trolley car, or grab an Uber, to ride through the city. It is the journey of a lifetime.

The Scholarship

The Twenty-Three bus rumbled up the cobblestones on Germantown Avenue bobbing Esther Jean Wayne's ninety-nine-pound body up and down like a puppet on a string.

"Bill. Slow down," she called out to the driver, already halfway into his daily round of gin.

The blistering sunlight poured like a rainstorm of harshness into her eyes. Her Dollar Tree sunglasses offered a modicum of protection. She needed prescription glasses but that cost money.

The letter she had received at her office, now in her purse, elated her. Her seventeen-year-old son, Marco, would escape their life in Germantown, escape the un-air-conditioned house, the drug infested neighborhood. His future was as bright as the gleaming sun. She had done her duty as a single mother. Thirty-four years old was not too late to start a new life.

The bus swerved to avoid a young black boy doing wheelies on his street bike. The biker flashed a mischievous smile at the bus driver. "Clarence, you are a damned fool," yelled Bill the driver.

The boy lifted the front wheel high, laughing, careless, reckless. "Stuff that bus," he called out.

"He's probably high on opioids," said Bill.

"It's a plague like the locusts in the Bible declared an elderly black man sitting across the aisle from her.

Esther Jean nodded, "Yes. I know Clarence Brown. He is a troubled boy. Bad families breed bad values. My Marco is better than that."

Bill rolled his eyes. "We all the same Ms. Esther. You are like your Biblical namesake who saved the Jews from slaughter. You want to save everybody. That their boy is toting a mess of drugs. Mo Mo has a small army of young boys riding around the City delivering drugs. And the cops know it. Their bread is well-buttered."

Esther sighed, a smile crossing her lips. Mo Mo could have his sons. She had her Marco.

The bus eased past Chelten Avenue and Vernon Park, a known night-time supermarket for drug deals despite the efforts of the Friends of Vernon Park to keep the Park a civilized community- friendly area. Drug dealers infested the Park like rats ravaging a carcass.

Her journey came to an end six minutes later as the bus slid to a stop near the Horrter Street bus stop.

"Here you are Ms. Esther," said the bus driver.

"Thank you, Bill."

She had moved onto Horrter Street right after Marco was born. She felt the enclosed porch offered a measure of protection from the criminal element headed by Maurice Montgomery, aka Mo Mo. The man stood six feet-six and weighed over two hundred and fifty muscular pounds. He could rip a phone book in half or crush an Adam's Apple with his fingers.

Mo Mo stood at the corner; his swarthy arms folded across his tight, black muscle tee shirt. His jean clad legs stood, planted wide on his black leather boots. His black eyes flashed at her, leering sex.

The sun glanced over his shaved head, casting him in a shadowy glow.

The devil.

"Hello Ms. Wayne. Y'all looking exquisite this evening. But you always look exquisite."

Clarence steered his bike close to the bus as it rounded the corner, his wheels squealing. He spun around Mo Mo, his youthful eyes aglow, wide and glassy.

He parked the bike and pulled an envelope from his jeans. "Mr. Mo Mo. Here is the envelope from the boys at the Park."

Mo Mo peeled a twenty dollar bill out of the roll in the envelope. "You did well, Clarence. I got another run for you."

He whispered into the boy's ear. Clarence stuffed the twenty into his jeans. Smiling, he gave Mo Mo a thumbs up and took off on his bike, heading north on Germantown Avenue.

He looked like any other twelve-year-old out for a bike ride.

Mo Mo smirked. "Drive safe, little man."

Esther stared at him defiantly. The man had clutched a lot of young boys in his fiendish grasp. He would not get his claws into Marco.

Esther lifted her chin and walked away, slowly, showing no fear though her insides roiled in anxiety from being two feet from Lucifer himself, a demon from her past.

She trod up the stone steps, pausing at the mailbox, envelopes jutting in the air unexpectedly. Marco had taken in the mail ever since he turned seven. Why not today? She collected the mail and let herself in, feeling apprehensive. She liked order and certainty.

The house was stifling hot. Marco always turned on the AC window units when he arrived from school. Where was he?

She laid the mail on her kitchen table and called Marco's cell phone. Her call went to voice mail.

"Marco. It's Mama. Where are you? Get home. I have something important I want to share with you. I will make your favorite meal tonight. Catfish and red beans and rice. Come home, Son."

Second-hand furniture filled the living room, dining room and kitchen like a rummage sale in Situ. Scrimping and flea markets and occasional trash picking, along with shopping at the Dollar Tree and not owning a car had kept the roof over their heads and food for the table. Marco had a ticket to a better life that fulfilled her dreams for him. Maybe he will become a Doctor. But that was a lot of schooling and tons of money. Same too with becoming a Lawyer or Dentist. No matter what it took, she would get her son through school and into a successful career. She changed into jeans and a Phillies tee shirt. The red shirt would hide any stains from the red sauce she was preparing. The recipe was handed down to her by her mother, a refugee from Mexico. Mother was at eternal rest.

She would have been proud of me and Marco.

An hour passed but no word from Marco. Concerned she called him again only to get voice mail. She texted him to call her.

Esther could not eat dinner. She filled a plastic container with the catfish, rice, and beans for another day. She turned on the music channel to smooth jazz, typically a remedy for her lifelong anxiety. Chris Botti's trumpet offered little relief. Had Marco done something stupid like that young boy who did wheelies around a bus?

Midnight arrived with no word from Marco.

She lay on the sofa and prayed to a god she had not worshipped in seventeen years.

Marco stepped through the front door at two am. His downturned mouth and glossy eyes alarmed her.

"Where have you been?"

Marco sat across from her on a sofa. He pulled off white and blue Nike sneakers. They were new to Esther.

"Where did you get those expensive sneakers?

"I bought them. "

"Where did you get the money?"

"From my new job. I am working for Mo Mo."

"What? Are you crazy?"

Marco pulled a wad of cash from his jeans. He spread the bills across the coffee table. "Here be three thousand dollars large. Take it and don't ask me any questions."

"How dare you talk to me like that. I am your mother."

"Yeah. And you are a liar, Mama."

"What?"

"You been lying to me for my whole damn life."

Esther's stomach tightened into a nugget of anxiety. "I never lied to you."

"Yeah you did."

An image from her past swept across her mind. Mo Mo.

Marco leaned forward, staring at her with a grimace she had never seen on his face. He was angry, hurt, and sad.

"Listen to me." She handed him the letter from her purse. "You won a National Merit $40,000 Scholarship. Ten grand a year for four years. Look at the letter and rejoice."

Marco read the letter and set it aside. "That is the second surprise this week. Guess what tops getting a full boat scholarship? M O N E Y."

"What are you talking about? You should be happy as hell. You have a ticket out of Germantown. You can become whatever you want to become.

I worked my butt off for you. I scrimped and saved and did without for you. And you look at me like I was a criminal. Like I was Mo Mo, not your Mama. You are breaking my heart."

Marco paced the room, staring alternately at Esther and the cash on the coffee table.

"Tonight, I met my father. He told me the truth."

Esther's jaw sank in disbelief.

Marco stood over her. "You told me my Father was a Marine, a hero killed in Afghanistan fighting the Taliban. The truth is Mo Mo is my daddy. He was married when he knocked you up. This be the truth. My Mama was a stinking whore. She screwed around with a married man. You lied to me. I owe you nothing. I will do as I want, and not what you want. You hear me, Mama. I am a man now. Mo Mo took me into his business like a father takes his son into a trade. I do not need to go some Uncle Tom college with a bunch of honkies. I am my own man."

Esther burst into sobs. "No, no. no. no, no."

"You lied Mama. You lied your whole damn life. That scholarship is for your pride, and not for my benefit. Fess up. You screwed up and lied to cover your tracks. You are not any better than Mo Mo. At least he told me the truth.

Esther gasped as her heart stopped for four seconds. Her head spun. She collapsed on her knees to the floor. Her eyes turned glassy and rolled back into her head. "Why God?" she said and passed out.

Esther awoke to Marco swabbing her face with a cold washcloth as she lay on the sofa. Marco's scowl had disappeared.

Behind him Mo Mo loomed like a specter from hell. "How are you feeling Mama?" asked Marco.

"I am okay Marco. Why is he here? Get that devil out of our home."

"No Mama."

"How is Miss Esther?" asked Mo Mo.

Esther sat up. "Get out."

Marco stood up. "Mo Mo has a plan. He needs a safe house. We let him do his business here and he pays us three thousand a week in cash. We live here as a family."

"No. This is our home, and not his safe house. We could all go to jail."

Mo Mo shook his head. "I got more cops on my payroll than you can imagine. The new DA dislikes cops. He wants nobody to go to jail. You and our boy can live here safe and rich. And you do not have to work a day for the rest of your life."

Esther curled her fists into two balls. "My house is not for sale. I am not a criminal and neither is my son. Now get out."

"If he goes, so do I," said Marco.

"The only place you are going is to a college. I am your mother and you will do as I say. Dammit Marco. I may have kept the truth from you, but I love you and you are a minor. If that monster gets his hooks into you, he will devour you. I will not let that happen. Now, am I clear."

"Be practical Esther. It is all for the best for everybody," said Mo Mo.

Esther shook her fist at Mo Mo. "Do not try that BS on me."

Marco looked at her pleading, yet defiant. "Listen to the man. Mo Mo is the Man. He is the father I never had. He will do right by us."

"God save me. I raised a fool. That beast eats people alive. He will take over our world. No, Marco. No. You must resist the temptation of that cash. Believe in yourself. Become a real man who walks the world with pride and honor. You are better than me and him. You are the future."

Marco shuffled his feet, glancing at Mo Mo and Esther. "Why did you lie to me?"

"Mothers often lie to protect their children. I lied to keep my sins off your soul. Forgive me, Lord Almighty."

Mo Mo put his arm around Marco. "It is time for you to be a man. Your own man. Stand with me and you will own the world, and be a slave to no man."

Marco squeezed Esther's hand. "I got to go with my father."

The next morning, she rose as usual. She showered and dressed as usual.

Over her morning tea, she read the Scholarship letter three times. She had to get to work. Maybe in a few days Marco would wise up. She made a mistake and survived. She would never give up her son. She slid it unfolded into her purse.

Esther walked down Horrter Street to Germantown Avenue. She had to cross the cobblestoned street lined with the old trolley tracks to catch the southbound bus. The bus was cruising toward her stop, and Bill was at the wheel, his hat pulled down tight, his eyes nearly shut.

She started across the Street when out of the corner of her eye she saw the boy Clarence on the bicycle doing a wheelie around a car stopped at the far corner. He whirled past the stopped car on one wheel. The bike tires lost traction on the rails. The boy flew off the bike landing on his back directly in the path of the incoming bus. Esther rushed across the street, picked up the boy and shoved him to safety. The bus wheels screeched.

"Bill cried out, "Miss Esther!!" The bus swerved and struck her full force, sending her headfirst down the street. The impact lofted her tiny body high into the air before landing hard against the cobblestones. Prone, her back broken, blood sliding down her cheeks, staring at the brilliant sun, she cried out, "Save Marcooooooo. God help me."

When Esther woke, her mind reeled in confusion. *Where am I?*

The line hung from a plastic bag into her right arm. Red and green lines spread across the computer screen. Numbers flashed, changing every few seconds. A hand gently touched her arm.

"Mama it is Marco. Are you okay?"

"Marco. O dear, sweet Jesus. Where am I?"

"You are in Chestnut Hill hospital. The doctors have been tending to you since the accident. That dang fool Clarence nearly got you killed. Mo Mo broke the fool's arms for you getting hurt. He made me find Clarence and then made me hold him while he yanked his arms from his sockets and twisted them until the bones snapped. It was not punishment. It was savageness. And Mo Mo was smiling the whole time like he was getting' off on inflicting the hurt on Clarence. I have never seen anything like that.

"I am so sorry," she said sobbing.

"Don't be sorry Mama. You did nothing wrong."

"I tried to save you. I tried to protect you from evil. I failed. Mo Mo will break your arms someday. Clarence is his son, too."

"My brother by another mother damn near got my mother killed?

Damn and double damn."

"I should have died. God help me die."

"Mama I learned today that drug money is easy money. It comes easy and goes easier. I can get money. But I only got one Mama and I damn near lost her because Clarence was high at eight in the morning. You know what Mo Mo said? Now you are mine. I knew he meant he owned me like a master owns a slave. He is death in life. He scared me to face the truth."

Marco knelt at her side. Tears drizzled down his smooth, brown cheeks, glistening like rain under the lights of the computer screens.

Marco pulled out the Scholarship letter. "Look here, Mama. You and I won a scholarship. Mo Mo had nothing to do with it. We did it without him. I can make it in this world without Mo Mo. But I cannot make it without you. Mama, I need you. You got to see me graduate someday."

Mo Mo's body filled the open doorway. "Get off your knees, boy. No son of mine kneels. Stand up like a man. And stop crying like a sissy. Your Mama ain't gonna die."

Marco stood, fists curled into tight balls. "Screw you Mo Mo. You do not scare me."

Mo Mo laughed out loud. "Boy, your Daddy needs to give you an ass whipping."

"Go for it," said Marco.

Mo Mo cracked a wide smile, a devil's smile. "Well, well, well. Esther done raised a brave man."

"Leave him alone," said Esther.

Mo Mo slid his belt from around his waist. "Bend over boy and take your whipping."

"No way!" yelled Marco. Mo Mo snapped the belt across Marco's shoulders.

"Ow. Stop that shit."

Mo Mo grinned wide, a surly, menacing smile. "Take your whipping, boy."

Esther pressed the emergency button at her side. "I called the orderlies. Now git Mo Mo, or they will lock your jive ass up," she said.

The red alarm blared. Blue lights flashed. A voice cam over the intercom. "Code blue in room eleven!"

Footsteps clambered down the hallway. Mo Mo raised his fist up and swung at Marco's head. The swing stopped an inch short of his face. Mo Mo held the fistic pose.

"Go home with your Mama. You ain't no son of mine."

Mo Mo shoved his way past the orderlies.

"What is going on?" asked the orderlies.

"Nothing," said Marco. "My mother just chased away a bad dream. She will be fine. She is a savior of her son, just like her namesake Esther in the Bible saved her nation. She saved me."

"Amen," said Esther. "Praise Jesus. My son is saved."

Marco laid the Scholarship letter on her bed.

"Mama. Which school should I attend?"

Esther bit her lip, holding back tears. "Any one!"

Esther reached her arm out. "Hug me, please. Just hug your Mama."

Unassuming Hero

On the morning of his seventy-fifth birthday, August third, 2019, Martin Schmidt followed his daily physical regimen of twenty pushups and fifteen pull ups with a brisk walk from his home in West Mount Airy on Allens Lane down the path along Cresheim Creek. He walked quickly to raise his pulse as his Cardiac Doctor had suggested.

Six and a half months ago, he had arrived by ambulance at Chestnut Hill hospital Emergency in time to beat the widow maker, a ninety-six percent closure of his main artery. A stent had been inserted into his wrist up to his heart. The dieting and the exercise routine had knocked off thirty-five pounds and reduced his waist size from forty to thirty-three. He felt proud of his accomplishment. Back in fighting weight.

He crossed the creek below the boyhood swimming hole named Dynamite based on a local legend that the waterhole was blasted into existence by kids playing with dynamite. The pool reflected his diminutive stature, balding head and wire-rimmed glasses.

Is that old man really me?

A disbelieving "yes" reverberated in his mind. It had to be him; no one else was in sight.

A warm breeze wafted through the oak trees surrounding the waterhole. A perfect morning for a man's birthday. His wife Grace, his four children, ten grand kids and two great grandsons planned to gather at his home for a celebratory birthday party cookout. He was proud he had built a strong family with only one divorce and no criminal records for the group. Imperfect but solid. Much like him, a lifetime insurance agent for Allstate.

His heart was heavy after reading the obituary that his hero, Edward "Fast Eddie" Moore was dead. Sixty years ago, Fast Eddie had taught him the lesson of a lifetime. He owed Eddie a priceless debt. Eddie had given him courage, the virtue that makes all virtues possible.

Martin tugged off his tan, lace-less Sketchers and settled his butt on a smooth rock at the water's edge and dangled his feet into the cool water. The water felt soothing. The old days were gone, just like Eddie. A new order had taken hold. He feared for the future of his family. They had prospects but no heroes; his high school, Cardinal Dougherty, once the largest Catholic High School in the country was now a charter school. Six of its priests had been named pedophiles, including that sadistic prick, Father James Dolan.

He should have brought his Phillies cap to shield the sun. Father Dolan was bald. Built like a tank with a husky torso and thick, muscular shoulders. Dolan had a unique way of torturing the students. He would order them to the gym after class where he would make them box him. He rarely boxed seniors. His prey were smaller freshmen and sophomores. He'd smash their faces in, watch them bleed and cry, all while laughing aloud, adding insult to injury.

Dolan grew up in Kensington, a neighborhood that inspired street kids to become junk yard dog tough and street smart. He tried a career in boxing but lacked the defensive skills needed to beat the better fighters. Though, he was a brawler with an iron chin and a killer instinct. He liked to hurt people. Rumors spread that he joined the priesthood to avoid serving in Korea. Some students believed his family doctor was a veterinarian.

Dolan taught typing and ran the gym. His students were mainly freshmen and sophomores. He also monitored the cafeteria. He would prowl the lunch tables like a vulture perusing a carcass, thirsty for bloody morsels. If a student talked too loudly or laughed too loudly, Dolan would smack the back of his head so hard the "thwack" would resound across the cafeteria, immediately silencing the hundreds of students. The other proctors never challenged him.

On December 26, 1960, the Philadelphia Eagles defeated Vince Lombardi's Green Bay Packers 17-13. The City celebrated for a year. It was an era of good feeling. But not for all students.

A week later, Martin sat next to table captain Eddie Moore, a black boy whose toothy smile would light up a cave. The lunch hour began at eleven fifteen. The menu was hot dogs, mashed potatoes, string beans, and white bread and butter. Martin and Eddie were engaged in a friendly disagreement over which coach was better, Lombardi or Buck Shaw. Martin favored Shaw because the Eagles had won.

Eddie's friendly smile flashed under his dark brown eyebrows. "Buck Shaw could not coach Cardinal Dougherty. The Eagles won because Van Brocklin ran the offence and Bednarik ran the defense. Old Buck puffed on a cigar and let the old pros manage the game."

"Lombardi lost. Period."

Eddie playfully punched Martin's shoulder. "You wanna take it outside, Little Man?"

"No way. You are older, bigger, and stronger. I prefer debating."

"Some fights you cannot debate your way out of, so you just have to take your whipping and keep on ticking."

Martin shrugged, not wanting to annoy Eddie. "I like debate."

The lunch bell rang. Martin picked up his tray, turned and bumped into Father Dolan's chest. The tray overturned, spilling trash down Dolan's cassock.

Martin turned as white as Dolan's collar. "Sorry Father. *Mea Culpa*."

Dolan's face screwed up into a mask of rage. He slapped Martin hard across his face. *"Thwack."*

His cheek flaming, Martin teared up. "I said I am sorry, Father. It was an accident. I am truly sorry."

Dolan loomed over Martin, grinning like a devil who had just seduced an angel. Spittle dripped from his lips. "I know you Schmidt, you are a wise ass. You need to be taught a lesson on carelessness. After eighth period, you will report to the gym for a boxing lesson."

Martin nodded, his stomach roiling in nausea. "Yes, Father Dolan.

Leering, Dolan patted his cheek. "Good boy," he said before he turned away, his broad back casting a sinister warning of evil. Martin felt a fear he had never known. The fear of helplessness.

Eddie grabbed Martin's arm. "Come with me. You need a boxing lesson."

Eddie led him into the men's room. "You got one chance to stay alive. When he charges you like a crazy bull, you drop down low and swing upwards and fire a right uppercut to his balls."

Martin stared wide-eyed, unsure, terrified. "That is a low blow. He'll really get mad."

Eddie shook Martin by his shoulders. "That is what I am hoping for. I will take over from there. Just make sure you do as I say. Got it?"

"Yes. Drop low and upper cut his nuts, and then get out of his way."

"We got no time to rehearse. Just do it."

"Why are you helping me?"

Eddie smiled, his eyes as wide as Broad Street. "I like you and I want a crack at that sick bastard."

"Won't you get into trouble?"

Eddie threw back his head. "I am a black Catholic in an all-white School who lives in a black, Baptist Community. I wake up and go to sleep in trouble. Now git to class."

Martin could not focus in class. He considered cutting out of the gym encounter. Dolan would track him down. He could not go to his Catholic parents. They would side with the priest. He had to trust Eddie. Maybe prayers would help?

The gym air was sweaty, hot and packed with the basketball team running drills. The overhead lights sprayed the hardwood floor with a glaring light as though the sun had been let in as a witness to Martin's pending date with Dolan.

Dressed in white gym shorts, a tee shirt, worn out black high-top sneakers, Martin entered and headed right to Eddie. Eddie wore gym shorts and a black sleeveless tee shirt. His taut muscular body gleamed like a young Adonis ready to do the work of the gods.

Dolan entered, striding like a gladiator, his arms swinging from his broad shoulders, two sets of boxing gloves hanging from his ham hock hands. Martin peered at the oncoming Goliath, wishing he had a sling shot and a sharp stone.

Somebody yelled, "Kick ass time."

The crowded gym turned quiet. The students formed a circle. Martin stepped into the circle like a condemned man going to the gallows. Dolan passed him the boxing gloves. "Put them on," ordered Dolan.

Eddie slipped the gloves over Martin's thin hands. "You got one shot. Make it count. I will do the rest."

Martin nodded, preferring to run rather than fight. "Okay."

Martin eyed Dolan's heavy gut and his crotch, hoping the arrogant priest did not wear a jock strap.

"Ding, ding, ding," said Dolan, sneering.

The priest rushed across the circle, his right arm cocked to deliver a knockout punch.

Martin crouched with his gloves held high. The onrushing bull was three feet away when Martin sank as low as a limbo stick. He fired his right hand into Dolan's shorts. He felt Dolan's genitals smash under his punch. Dolan's eyes popped sky high as he let out a vicious howl, like a hurt wolf.

Martin skirted away towards Eddie. Eddie jumped into the circle. "Foul. Foul. Martin loses. Father Dolan wins by disqualification." Eddie tore off Martin's gloves.

Dolan wheezed. "Put those gloves back on that twerp. I will kill him."

Eddie put on the gloves. "If you want a fair one, try me."

Dolan nodded. "You asked for it boy."

Dolan took a deep breath, shook his shoulders and moved toward Eddie. Eddie snapped a jab that stopped Dolan in his tracks. He followed with a right cross that split Dolan's lip. Dolan's eyes glared hate. He swung wildly. Eddie ducked and landed a hard right to Dolan's gut. He whipped a left hook to Dolan's jaw and then a left-right cross combination to Dolan's nose. The right broke Dolan's nose. Dolan blinked like he had been blindsided by a runaway truck. Eddie landed a second combination to Dolan's jaw. The priest landed on his butt as the crowded gym erupted into laughter and applause.

"Dolan getting whipped," a boy chanted. The whole gym repeated over and over. "Dolan getting whipped. Dolan getting whipped. Dolan getting whipped."

Dolan rose, blood pouring down his face, chin dripping onto his shirt. He whirled like a dervish, sneering.

"Dolan getting whipped," yelled the chorus.

Dolan walked away, his head bowed, whimpering. "You bastards will all pay."

Eddie took Martin by the arm. "Never concede to a bully. Never."

Martin bobbed his head in gratitude.

"I will never do that."

"Kid, you never lose a fight unless you quit."

Martin trudged up the hill. His family awaited. He'd raised them to be brave, to fight evil. To never give in. They were his legacy of a lifetime of work and winning the small battles that make one's life worth living. He'd preached and practiced the adage that evil prevails when good men do not intervene. Eddie had made him a man. Eddie had been right about Lombardi, too. Eddie knew a winner when he saw one. Dolan was later named as a pedophile in a list printed in the Inquirer in the eighties. He had a corner reserved for him, in hell.

Martin stopped at the top of the hill, above the tree line. The creek poured downstream carrying memories of his youth. He sweated like a boxer after a twelve-round match. *Which round am I in?*

"God bless you Fast Eddie. You made the world a better place."

The Gang's All Here

It is February 4, 2018, a day that will live in Philadelphia history. The Eagles are underdogs in the Super Bowl against the New England Patriots. The Eagles are underdogs, just like the City, and the Mayfair section of Philly is a giant sports cave. Men and women and children of all ages are glued to their televisions. The clock winds toward six-thirty PM. The anticipation rises to a frenzy in McGarrity's tavern, a shot and beer bar on Frankford Avenue just south of Cottman Avenue in Mayfair.

The fans sitting in the sixteen seats at the bar and two rows behind them all wear green sweatshirts. Eagles fans sing the national anthem with Pink, Doylestown born. To the many who have bet on the underdog Eagles, the choice of a Philly area girl to sing the anthem is a sign God took the points and bet the Eagles.

Jerry Malloy, born and raised in Mayfair, stretches his Spanx shirt over his beer belly. He needs to look younger and trimmer if he is to attract Maeve Corbett. Jerry has had a life-long crush on the diminutive strawberry blond with piercing, bright blue eyes and freckles across her alabaster skin. He dares not let his ball-busting buddies discover his secret. He pats the sides of his torso, feeling handsome, thin and worthy of Maeve's attention.

He hustles down Frankford Avenue and barges into the crowded bar just as Pink finishes the anthem. Maeve sits on a barstool, a bottle of Yuengling in front of her and the scoundrel Rory Shea next to her. Jerry detests Rory for his cheating ways on Jerry's cousin Lisa.

Jerry elbows his hefty body through the crowd to a corner of the bar. Jerry slaps two twenties on the bar. He waves at Nick McGarrity tending bar. "The usual if you please?"

Nick McGarrity pours a Guinness. "Here ye be, Jerry."

"Thanks. Back up, Maeve."

"Done."

Maeve turns to him with a bright smile. "Thanks Jerry."

"We are gonna kick Brady's butt," says Jerry.

"Did you bet on the game?" asks Maeve.

"Fifty to win and fifty for the over."

"Smart bet," says Rory.

Jerry hoists his pint and toasts the portrait of Mayfair's hero and benefactor, the late Augustine Mahon. "Mr. Mahon is looking down on us. He will have a word with God and bring us home a win."

"I said a Hail Mary at Mass today," says Maeve.

"My sainted mother said a rosary," says Jerry.

Rory leans close to Maeve, leering like a letch.

The Eagles jump out in front. The bar roars as the Eagles build a twelve-point lead, 15-3.

The crowd chants, "E A G L E S, Eagles!!"

Jerry buys a round of shots for himself and Maeve, and skips Rory. "Slainte," he says.

Jerry throws down a shot of Tullamore Dew. Maeve matches him. Rory opts for a double of John Powers. Rory is a bad drunk. Whiskey doubles his size and urge to fight.

The bar is hot. Jerry sweats under his Spanx. The sweating shaves pounds and inches. She is worth the ordeal.

He loved her at first sight, six years ago when she moved into Mayfair. She was married to Eddie O'Toole who was killed in a car accident. Eddie was driving drunk and high on opioids. She deserved better than Mayfair. He wants to get her out of the neighborhood.

Jerry is feeling good about his bets. The Eagles are getting five and a half points. The over bet is forty-seven. By halftime, the Eagles lead by double digits and the two teams have scored thirty-four points. The bet looks safe.

Justin Timberlake delivers a rocking halftime show. He performs "Until the End of Time" and "I Would Die for You" in a tribute to Prince. He closes the show with "Can't Stop the Feeling." Jerry feels flush. The hot bar and whiskey and Spanx shirt has him sweating profusely. He dares not leave her or take off his Jersey.

Mr. Mahon's portrait seems to sneer at him. Rory has a hand on Maeve's knee. Jerry wants to punch him square in his smile.

Timberlake dances into the stands. The Minneapolis stadium dances with him. The bar erupts into a dance fest. Maeve leaps up and grabs Rory's hand. "Dance with me," she says.

She bobs up and down and swings her arms from side to side. Her breasts bounce under her Carson Wentz jersey. Rory ogles her like a wolf ready to pounce on a lamb.

Jerry pushes his way to the men's room. He pees in a stall to hide the Spanx. Finished, he splashes cold water from the sink on his face. The mirror reveals a thirty-year-old man with puffy cheeks and blood shot eyes. Nausea creeps into his gut.

What a sorry mess you are.

The dancing is over. Rory is chatting up Maeve. The second half is about to begin. Jerry wants to grab Rory by his balls and throw him out of the bar.

The Eagles keep the pressure on, but the Patriots ere not about to give up. The Patriots took a 33-32 lead. The bar crowd grumbles in disbelief. Coach Pederson plays to win, unlike other Eagles coaches who play to not lose. The Eagles soar back into the lead with a field goal. The two-point lead is too thin, too precarious against Brady, the best quarterback of all time.

The Patriots go on a sustained drive. Near their goal line, the Eagles switch positions on their defensive line. The move causes confusion in the offensive blocking assignments. The Eagles defensive end crashes into Brady. Tom Terrific fumbles. The crowd senses this play is the turning point. The bar chants, "E A G L E S."

Jerry joins in, chanting in unison with Maeve. It feels good to share the moment with her.

The Eagles drive the length of the field, but the drive stalls inside the Patriots ten-yard line. The crowd fears Pederson will kick a field goal, leaving the Patriots with a chance to win the game. Pederson calls the now famous Philly play a fake reverse ending in a pass from tight end Trey Burton to Eagles quarterback Nick Foles. The played works. Foles catches the pass in the end zone. The Eagles are Super Bowl Champs. And Jerry has won his two bets.

Happy pandemonium breaks out. Maeve hugs him. She pulls away, a quizzical smirk on her face. "What are you wearing under your jersey?"

"A tee shirt," he says.

She giggles aloud, "Really. You have a girdle on. You plump man you. Do you need a bra too?"

Embarrassed, he heads to the restroom. When he comes back, he finds a shot on the bar courtesy of the house. He throws it down under the watchful eyes of the Mahon portrait. Mr. Mahon is a Philly legend. He'd been a political leader, owner of the City's largest paving company and City Sheriff. Jerry is a two-hundred-forty-pound slug in a girdle.

The celebration pours outside into the streets of Mayfair. The citizenry climb light poles, dance on the roofs of cars, set off firecrackers, ring cowbells and chant over and over, "E A G L E S!"

The bartender joins the celebration. Alone in the bar, an old ditty crosses Jerry's mind. His father and his friends would sing it on many a Friday night at the tavern.

He sings aloud, his nasally off-key voice echoing across the empty bar, with tears welling in his baby blue eyes. He has lost Maeve forever. And his dignity.

"Hail, hail, the Gangs all here
What the hell do we care?
Why the hell should we care?
What the hell do we care, now?"

You Never Know

Kenny Hale sat across from Beatrice, Beatie, his wife of thirty-six years. The Christmas presents stood piled under the artificial tree he'd bought at Walmart on Cheltenham Avenue, near his twin brick home on Mount Pleasant Avenue. The Christmas lights blinked alternately red, white, and green, changing, in flux, just like he had been all day. He needed money. Steady income to add to their Social Security payments. Kenny did not want to work for anyone else. Thirty-four years at Aramark as a warehouseman had diluted his appetite for bosses and rules.

"Beatie. I have been thinking about driving for Uber. It is easy money for an old man. You get paid every day and only work when you feel like it. We can use the extra kale."

"Kenneth Nathan Hale, you are not a very good driver. Your eyes do not work well after dark. And you have the patience of a scared pigeon. Get yourself a part-time job at Walmart, or Acme, or Giant."

Kenny ran his thin forefinger against his thick, black and gray right eyebrow. "I would not be happy behind a cash register or stocking shelves. Nope. I am going to try Uber."

"For gosh sakes. You cannot drive at night. Do not be a stubborn fool. I bet your car insurance will go up, too."

"Yes, it will. I checked with Joe Hussery at Allstate. I figured gas mileage. I can clear twenty-five an hour. Working twenty hours a week, that comes out to five hundred a week. We can use that dough."

Beatie frowned over her grey framed glasses. "Seems like you thought through the numbers. Did you ever think about the risks?" Beatie folded her arms across her chest, a sign she had a knockout punch to deliver on his ego.

"What risks?"

"You never know who is going to get into that car with you."

"That is part of the appeal. I will get to meet people from all walks of life. I like that. Tell you what. I will try it for a couple of months to see how it goes."

Beatie laughed. "You old fox. You used that line to get me to date you for the first time."

"It worked, didn't it?"

"Yes, it did. My man will be the Uber man. Go on ahead and try it."

Kenny walked to her and kissed her cheek. "I will make you proud of me."

"Hmmm. Didn't your Mama tell you not to get into a car with a stranger?"

"I can take care of myself."

"Wait until I tell the family. They will be amused that their Daddy is finally living in the twenty-first century."

Kenny took out his flip phone. "Tomorrow I trade this baby in for an Apple iPhone. Ain't that a hoot?"

Beatie shook her head, smiling. "You are a hoot, for sure."

Kenny felt like a young boy who just learned how to ride a bike.

On an early Saturday morning in March, Kenny went online, reluctantly. The first week turned into a disconcerting time, a nightmare of App navigational failures, cranky riders, and few tips. His rating remained high at 4.9 but the one-star ratings irked him. He suspected that the Uber Pool riders blamed him for poor navigation to pick up points. His earnings hovered around twenty dollars per hour. Beatie sensed his dissatisfaction. He dared not admit she may be right.

The App resounded with a call in Chestnut Hill on Evergreen Avenue. Chestnut Hill was a well-to-do neighborhood at the edge of northwest Philly. Rides tended to be longer and more lucrative. And they tipped.

The rider was a thirty something white woman dressed in designer jeans, a black leather jacket. Her blond hair was swept back behind her. A Nordic goddess.

The screen read her name, "Elsa."

Kenny cast his best smile. "Good morning Elsa. I am Kenny."

"Hello. This will be a round trip," she said matter-of-factly.

"Sure. No problem. I like round trips."

The destination surprised him. It was to Kensington Avenue near Allegheny Avenue, the heart of the drug trade in Philly.

The Chevy Cruze LT wound down Lincoln Dive and then Ridge Avenue through the North Philly mean streets towards Kensington. Kenny felt that an early morning trip was probably safe. Who does a car jacking before breakfast? Uber had a 911 emergency button on the App.

He arrived at the destination', a side street lined with row homes. Elsa called out, "Pull over by that open space over there and wait."

Ahead, a group of ten or more guys dressed in jeans and hoodies or sweatshirts lounged in front of a rundown home. One white man pulled on a joint casually. He waved Elsa to come to the house. She skipped up the steps and into the house.

Kenny kept his eyes peeled. One of the men approached the Cruze. He was Hispanic, sharp black eyes, tattoos on his throat and hands. His hoodie hung loosely on his shoulders like a shroud.

"Nice wheels," he said.

"Yeah, I like it."

"You must do okay with this Uber gig."

"I make a few bucks. How are you doing?"

The man cracked a snaky smile, flashing bright, sharp incisors, like fangs. "I do great. Lots of money. Lots of women. Lots of everything."

Elsa skipped down the steps and strode toward the car. "Get inside, Carlo. Javier does not like you talking to strangers."

Carlo 's nostrils widened. "I do not take orders from women."

"Javier gave the order, not me. Go tell him."

Carlo sauntered away, glancing back at Elsa with a lascivious smile.

Elsa leaned into the car. "Go to the corner. Turn left and pull over to wait for me."

"Yes Ma'am." He said like a schoolboy facing a teacher.

Kenny found a spot to park. Elsa walked by him and stepped into another home. He waited with the car running and the doors locked. Sweat caked his shirt, front and back.

When Elsa reappeared, her sweater bulged at her midriff. She was carrying a large package.

"Home," she said, her voice calm, a smirk twisting her lips.

Kenny drove back, careful not to draw attention. He passed a parked Police squad car but did not look at the two patrolmen.

Thirty-six minutes later, he arrived on Evergreen Avenue.

Elsa got out. "Thanks for your service."

"Bye, Elsa."

Kenny went offline. He drove home badly in need of a break and a cup of coffee and a moment with Beatie. He would not tell her about the trip lest she fear he was in danger. He would eat lunch and go out later. He needed the money. He needed time to sort out what happened on the trip to hell.

Kenny got a pick-up call at two fifteen. The voice called out. "Evergreen Avenue. Pick up Elsa."

He had never had a repeat rider in the same day. Was it a coincidence or fate? He headed to her home anxious to see what fate had in store for him.

Elsa emerged from her home dressed in a white nurse's uniform. She carried a large leather satchel.

"Twice in one day," said Kenny as she entered the car.

"Get moving or I will be late for work."

Her destination was Einstein Hospital on Broad Street.

Kenny drove in silence, afraid to draw her attention. How could he get her as a passenger twice?

He drove feeling nervous, nauseous, scared. The trip ended on Broad Street. Elsa threw a five-dollar bill onto the passenger side front seat.

"Have a *quiet* day," she said.

He immediately went offline. His heart was pounding. She was part of a drug deal.

Telling Uber would cost him his job. Ratting out Elsa would cost him his life. He needed a shower and a nap to clear his head.

Kenny barely touched dinner. He needed the red wine more than the fried chicken and noodles.

Beatie was in a good mood. Her hair hung long over her shoulders. She wore a pearl necklace above her tight sweater. Kenny tried to smile. He tried to laugh when she laughed. He was too scared to feel passion, a first in their marriage.

"I am so glad we have time to ourselves. I may even get romantic tonight," she said.

A hard rap on the front door broke the moment.

"I'll get it," said Kenny.

A second hard knock was followed by three letters he never heard before in person. "F B I."

Beatie grabbed Kenny's shirt. Her eyes bulged with fear. "What the hell did you do?"

Kenny eased her hands from his shirt. "Nothing. I did nothing wrong."

Two FBI Agents entered, each dressed in dark suits, striped ties and shiny black, laced shoes. The taller black agent peered down at Kenny. "I am Special Agent Cornelius Williams. My associate is John Pascarella. We need to ask you a few questions about a female rider you drove this morning."

The Agents settled into the sofa. Kenny claimed his recliner after getting a kitchen chair for Beatie.

"Does my husband need a lawyer?" asked Beatie, arms folded across her chest in a defensive pose.

"Ma'am, we are seeking information regarding an ongoing investigation into a drug ring operating in Philly. Your husband may be able to help us."

"How can he help you? He drives for Uber?"

"Today he picked up a woman named Elsa Shimkus, a Polish immigrant, and drove her to two locations. We know the locations. We need additional information. He is not suspected of any criminal activity. To protect all parties, Agent Pascarella will tape this meeting. Mr. Hale, please look at this photo. Did you see this man at the Kensington location?"

Kenny lifted the photo. "Yes, Elsa called him Carlo."

The Agent showed him a second photo.

"I did not see this man. She did refer to a man named Javier as being the boss."

Agent Williams snapped his fingers. "This man is Javier Vasquez."

FBI agent Pascarella made a note on his iPhone. "Check."

"On the second trip, did she go to Einstein Hospital on Broad Street?"

"Yes. Only she was wearing a nurse's uniform. On the first trip she wore normal street clothes. Jeans, a top. And she carried this big bag. Wait. When she came out of the second house, she did not have the bag?

"Where was the second house located?"

"Around the corner. She went in with it and came out empty-handed. But her top was bulging like she had stuffed something under her sweater."

"Can you remember anything else about the trip that may be relevant?"

Kenny glanced at Beatie who looked frightened and angry. "No, but my wife Beatie warned me, you never know who is getting into your car. You were right, Beatie."

Agent Williams leaned close to Kenny. "You must keep this discussion confidential for your own safety. These people are very dangerous. We are close to nabbing them."

"Should I leave town or quit driving Uber?"

"No. They use Uber because they always get different drivers for each trip. Getting you twice in the same day defies all odds. Elsa probably did not say a thing fearing they will get scared and take it out on her."

"I see. I am not a hero. I will keep my trap shut."

Beatie shook her head. "No, I want more protection. I want police protection around the clock."

Pascarella put up a warning finger. "With all respect Mrs. Hale. You do not want a police car outside your home. It will draw attention, and if the Press or Media get wind there is an investigation, they will surround your home looking for News."

Kenny took Beatie's hand in his. "He's right. We will be fine."

Williams and Pascarella stood up. "Thanks for helping us. We will see our way out. Here is my card. Call me day or night," remarked Williams.

"Me too, and here's mine," added Pascarella.

Kenny locked the door behind them, feeling he was locking himself into a cell in his own home.

"Damn. All I did was drive a car."

Beatie wrapped her arms around him. "Hold me Kenny. Hold me."

Later, they made love with the intensity neither had felt in years. They fell asleep in each other's arms, feeling warm but afraid.

Kenny woke and headed to the shower ahead of Beatrice. He stood under the warm water thinking fate had played an evil trick on them.

He dressed and started the four cup Keurig. Beatie liked strong coffee. He found a loaf of rye bread and put four slices in the toaster on "Dark."

Beatie came into the kitchen wearing a robe, her hair wrapped in a towel.

"Beatie Girl. You look like Cleopatra."

"She's dead. What the hell are we going to do?"

Kenny poured her coffee into her favorite flowery cup, porcelain decorated with red roses against a pale- yellow background. He filled his Eagles mug. He placed the Coffee Mate and sugar in front of her.

"Thanks, Kenny. Now answer my question. What the hell are we going to do?"

Kenny laid his iPhone on the table.

"When I was ten, the white kids bullied me to stay out of the playground. When I was twelve, the Slocum Street gang bullied me to join them. I said no. They beat me up, but I did not join them. Now, I am fifty-two. I am too old to run or fight or be bullied. I am going to drive my car for a couple of hours each day to make some coin. You and I are going to brunch around noon. How about Michael's diner on Easton Road? You like their omelets."

She clasped his hands. "Damn if you are not a brave fool."

Kenny kissed the back of her hand. "You make me brave. If I can stand up to your bullying, these jokers are nothing." Beatie picked up his iPhone and pressed the Uber icon. The phone flashed, "You are now online."

"Drive safe Kenny. You never know who is getting into your car."

"Aye aye, Captain Beatie."

The Family Business

South Philly Sam Buono fastened his money belt under his black leather Jacket. His designer jeans were getting tighter. Fifty-two years of eating pasta, sausage, capicola, salami, provolone, cheesesteaks and hoagies widen the midriff while clogging the aorta. He had two stents to prove the dietary effects on the heart of processed deli and fatty foods.

He clambered down the second-floor steps of his two-story, red brick townhouse on Hulsemann Street, four blocks west of the Philly stadiums on Broad Street in South Philly. His Takoma western boots lay waiting at the bottom of the steps. The boots made him two inches taller, and his broad shoulders and no neck physique made him more imposing.

His wife Rita sat at the kitchen table, her back to the sunlit window. She was still a pretty woman though age had thickened her arms and legs. But her face glowed under the sunshine. There is still a lot of life in her, he mused.

He stuffed his twenty-two pistol in his rear waistline. He slid his "book" of gambling customers and bets into his back pocket. The Book was his livelihood, his business. Gamblers were coded by type of bet, amount bet, date, odds, winnings and losses. His points of betting origin were bars, private Clubs, and individuals via phone. No emails or texts allowed. Too easy to track.

"Do you want I should make you oatmeal?" she asked matter-of-fact, like a waitress at a diner.

Sam sat at the head of the table. "What I want is sausage, peppers and three eggs in a frittata. But the Doctor wants me to change, so I will eat oatmeal."

"It's good for you. I will brew you a coffee from the Keurig."

"Throw in an end slice of the Amoroso bread with a little butter."

Rita frowned. "Sure. No sugar in the coffee and you must use skim milk."

"Yeah, yeah, yeah. I see Anthony is still asleep. When did he get done driving Uber?"

"He got home at three am. He needs to find a better job."

"I know. I want to talk to him about that very situation. We can all talk at dinner tonight."

"What are you talking about?" she asked stern-faced as a cop making an arrest.

"The business is what. This heart thing got me thinking that I need a succession plan. He's twenty years old. Time for him to man up."

Rita stirred the pot of oatmeal, her eyes riveted to Sam's. "He has his own life to live. Let him find his own way."

"We are a family. My father and grandfather held onto the route for decades. We need to ensure that the tradition is carried forward. And we need the cash flow for the future. Be glad we only have one kid to worry about."

Rita pursed her lips to hold in words she wanted to spill out. If Sam only knew the truth.

Rita set the oatmeal and toasted Italian bread and coffee in front of Sam.

"Thanks," he said. He reached out his hand, but she pretended to not see it.

"I am going to take a shower," she said, wanting to avoid talking to him.

"Stay. Talk to me."

Rita folded her arms across her chest, bra-less under her Eagles tee shirt.

"You never listen to me, so why should I talk?"

"I listen. I just don't always agree. A man has got to do what he thinks is right for his family."

"Getting his twenty-year-old son involved in bookmaking is not my idea of doing the right thing for the family."

He took a tablespoon to his mouth feeling like a child eating what his mother put in front of him with no say so allowed. Sam blew on his oat meal. "Hot."

Rita started to walk away but turned, her face drawn into a painful scowl. "You talk about family but refuse to wear a wedding ring. You make me sick."

Sam pointed his spoon at her, jabbing the air three times. "I told you that wearing a ring is not conducive to collecting from guys that owe me. They see a ring and immediately see me as a man who is under a woman's thumb. The deadbeats look for any edge, any sign of weakness or softness. The ring is a no go in my business."

He threw the spoon into the sink. "That's enough of the baby food. I am going to the Penrose diner. I need real food."

Rita curled her fists into hard balls of anger. "Screw you Sam. Kill yourself with your stubborn Dago pride. Keep my boy out of your lousy business. Or else?"

Sam stood nose to nose with Rita. "Or what? You gonna call the cops? Hell, half the District is in my book. Go take your shower and calm down. I'll see you later."

He wheeled away, anxious to eat a three-egg omelet with hot sausage, home fries, well done rye toast, butter and jelly on the side. And coffee with two sugars. And no nagging.

He hopped into his black, 2019 Cadillac Escalade and roared off to the diner. His license plate read, AUSEM. "Always use somebody else's money."

It was Monday, pay off and collect day on pro football bets. The favored Eagles had lost and did not cover the Over bets. He could smell the money.

Halfway through eating his omelet, Sam motioned for the waitress to pour a second cup of coffee. He liked being waited on by a smiling, younger woman. He'd tip her well.

The diner was packed from counter to booths. A large, familiar figure approached him. He wore a grey fedora, thick, wire-rimmed glasses that reflected under the glaring overhead lights. John Carozzi was a made-man and the Captain of Sam's gambling ring. He had seventeen Earners on the Street. All feared the man. John was Rita's first cousin on her mother's side. In South Philly, everybody is related. Had she called him about Anthony?

"Hello John," said Sam.

"Buon giorno, Sam. They shook hands and John sat down. The Manager of the diner raced over carrying a pot of espresso and a porcelain cup. He poured John an espresso and bowed before hurrying away. John sipped it and smiled at Sam. Sam knew the smile was a deflection. John did not often meet with his earners one on one.

"How is your breakfast?" asked John.

"Good. The omelets here are the best in the city."

"I am glad I happened in here. I need to talk with you."

"What's up?"

"How is my cugina, Rita? Are you treating her well?"

"Of course. We have been married for over twenty years."

"It's a shame you two had only the one boy."

"She had a miscarriage. Her ability to have more was cut out. God's will."

"God acts in mysterious ways. I like clarity. Confusion is not good for business."

John twisted his massive ring on his right hand. The massive ring bore the head of a lion. Sam knew it was a subtle reminder of John's ability to hurt people. Sam had seen John smash his fist into the mouth of a dead beat. The man would eat oatmeal for the rest of his life for not paying up on a two-hundred-dollar bet.

"I will come directly to the point. Since you had that heart problem, your earnings have dropped twenty percent. Certain people think you are slowing down, so maybe your route needs to be lessened. Maybe one of the younger guys can step in to help you?"

Sam held his breath before answering. "Boss, you are a fortune teller. I planned on meeting with you to discuss an expansion plan. I am adding resources. I want your permission to add Anthony to my Book. He would be joining the family business. He can do the rounds while I find new customers. If we need muscle, I can still handle any difficulties. Is that okay with you?"

John twisted the ring. One straight right could knock a grown man down with a broken jaw.

John's forehead creased as he squinted through the coke bottle glasses. "You want to bring your kid on board? Is my godchild up for operating a Book?"

"I will bring Anthony along, with your permission. In six months, we will grow the earnings. And we will be keeping it in the family."

John poured a dash of sugar into his espresso." You have been with the family all your life. Your old man and his old man put in their years as earners. But these kids today are different. They lack respect. They want Socialism. What we do is pure entrepreneurship. No guarantees. Maybe think it over and we can talk further. Let's talk tomorrow. Here. Ten am."

"Absolutely."

John walked away leaving Sam feeling that he was just thrown off a boat into the ocean without a life jacket. His appetite followed John out of the diner. Sure as hell, Rita had called John. Damn.

The waitress stopped at his table. "Mr. Carozzi took care of your check and my tip. Do you need more coffee?"

"Only if you put a shot of VO in it."

"I can do Sambucca on the house."

"Too much sugar. Ah, screw it. Make it a double."

His head ached. The room seemed very warm, like a closet. He scanned the crowded diner. Once it was an all Italian diner. Now there were Koreans, Blacks, Vietnamese patrons. They were laughing, chattering in Spanish, Chinese and English all at once. The cacophony resounded like a discordant choir singing different tunes at once. When had the world changed so much?

He texted Anthony. "See you at home late tonight. Important. Love, Dad."

He started the route at Murphy's bar, a shot and beer hole in the wall. The clientele usually started drinking by seven am. Fuzzy O Donnelly owed him three hundred. Fuzzy was a Vietnam Vet who left part of his mind in Pleiku in 1974.

Fuzzy paid up. Sam stuffed the money in his jeans and made the notation in his Book. At Carney's Pub, he paid out fifty to Stuart Klein, a smart Jewish tailor who usually bet against the Eagles. By eleven am, the Eagles bettors had paid up twenty-one hundred. He was up over two grand. John would be happy, hopefully. He trudged through the route finally settling at Guppy's bar. A shot and beer joint known for hosting bachelor parties upstairs.

His heart was racing. He sat at the bar, waiting for George O Malley who lost five hundred on the Eagles. O Malley was a tough ex-Cop. He'd been forced off the Police after he assaulted a superior officer, a black man politically connected to Mayor Kenney. The newspapers and media made O Malley look like a KKK wizard.

O Malley strode into the tavern. He stood at the bar, ordered a shot of John Powers Irish whiskey and a mug of Miller beer. Jake the bartender served him and moved aside quickly.

A middle-age black woman sat across from O Malley. Her purple halter top showed a rack that a pole dancer would kill for. Her dangling gold earrings flashed across the room. She was advertising and available.

O Malley turned to Sam, his red hair flaming under the overhead lights. "If you came to collect, I don't have the money. Come another day."

Sam was not sure he could beat a payment out of a man twice his size. He pulled his gun. "Pay me now or I blow your foot off."

O Malley sneered, "You don't got the balls, Wop."

"Easy lads," said Jake.

"I thought you was Irish. But you are a Welsher sure as the sun shines in Italy," said Sam.

Sam put away the gun. A shooting would bring the police. John Carozzi would not like the publicity. "My friend Guppy O Leary deserves better patrons than a poof like you. My Boss, John Carozzi handles special cases. Tell him Jake. Tell him about John C."

Carney leaned his bony elbow on the bar. "O Malley, pay the man before he sets a wolf on you the likes of which would scare Satan skinny."

O Malley sneered. "I fear no man, especially Wops."

Sam laughed out loud. "Wops. You call us Wops. The man says we are men without papers. Hah. That's a term I have not heard in years." Sam held out his hand. "Let's shake. The Mick and the Wop."

He got within arms-length of O Malley before he launched a kick into the big man's balls. O Malley slumped forward to his knees. Sam crashed a hard right to O Malley's nose, breaking it instantly. Blood spurted from O Malley's nostrils. Sam grabbed O Malley's red hair and yanked him to the floor.

"Now who is getting whopped?"

Sam reached into O Malley's jeans and pulled out a wad of hundred-dollar bills.

"You chintzy loser. You had the cash all along."

Sam punched him in the mouth. "You are done, O Malley. No one will take your bets."

Sam counted out five Benjamins. "Jake. Bear witness, that I only took the five hundred clams which is owed me."

"You are an honest Bookie. All say so."

Sam felt a sense of satisfaction, a climax. All South Philly and John Carozza would hear about how he took down O Malley. His reputation would grow.

Sam took another hundred and laid it on the bar. "Tell the boys the drinks are on O Malley with my compliments."

"Indeed. You are a fine and generous man Sam," said Jake.

Sam's heart was pounding hard and fast. Panting, he reached the Escalade, worried that he was getting too old for the business. The kid had to chip in if he was going to survive in South Philly. He texted Anthony. "See you soon. Need your help. Love, Dad."

Stealing a parking space in South Philly is a declaration of war, especially if the owner dug out the snow. Everybody knows the protocol. Sam cursed at the Executive grey Cadillac in front of his house. The License plate read, "JOHNCAR 1."

John Carozzi had filled his spot. Incensed at the slap in his face, Sam circled the block four times before settling into a spot on Packer Avenue. The three-block walk to his house exercised his heart and his temper.

He collected himself and entered his home feeling that John was sending him a message. He trudged ahead, over seven grand in his pocket and his book in hand. Rita sat next to John who sat at the head of the table,

Sam's chair. Rita smiled not in greeting but in contempt. John did not rise to greet him. A sign of disrespect and trouble.

Sam stood at the side of the kitchen table. The moonlight cast the kitchen in a shadow.

"Hello Sam. Please sit down."

Sam tossed the money on the table.

"I earned over seven Gs today. The least I deserve is to sit in my own chair in my own kitchen."

John did not budge. "A chair is a chair. We need to talk about today."

"Where is Anthony?"

"He is at my mother's house."

"I told him to be here. I am his father."

Rita pounded her fist on the butcher block table. "I am his mother. I told him why you wanted to see him. I told him his future was to be a penny ante bookie. He declined."

Sam reeled as if she had shot him. "My son would never disrespect me. You are lying."

"She is telling you the truth. Now, sit down and listen to me and Rita," said John.

Sam spun a chair around and sat his with his arms folded over the back of the wooden chair. His blood pressure rose as high as the full moon.

"What the hell is going on here?"

John pointed a meaty finger at Sam. "You screwed up big time. You took down an ex-cop who is also a veteran and a second cousin to the Mayor. Worse, the whole beat down is recorded on the security camera in Guppy's and witnessed by an undercover female officer on under cover duty. You are dead meat Sammy boy."

"The black broad at the bar. She was a cop? Damn."

"Yes, you knucklehead. We live in 2020. Everybody is on camera. You think we live in the Sixties or the forties. You are out of tune with today. You are a liability. Now hand over your book."

Sam rose and reached his hand to his handgun. "No way. I built the Book. It is my life's work. I am not giving it up."

"Is your precious Book worth dying for?"

Sam nodded, his lower lip quivering in rage and fear. "A man has his pride. You sit in my chair. You took my parking space. Now you want the Book. Kiss off, John."

"Here is the deal. We buy out your half of the house for a hundred and fifty grand. You go to the shore. You get a pension equal to ten percent of the earnings. Take it or leave it."

"Just like that you snap your fingers and I disappear. What happens to Rita and Anthony?"

Rita laughed. "I am the big winner. I get a no contest divorce. Anthony goes to Penn State to study Business courtesy of the Family."

"I am out like a bag of trash."

"That is one way to look at it. Take the deal Sammy," said John. "Now hand me the Book."

Sam scanned the kitchen. "We had a home here. We had a tradition. We had a family business. We had it all. Why Rita? Why toss me away like the trash?"

"For over twenty years, you treated me like your maid. I had enough. Now get out of my house."

"What about Anthony?"

"My son is my son and he stays with me. Leave him alone."

"You cruel bitch. All I did for you. This is how you repay me."

Rita slapped him hard. "You want to know what I did. I did not have a miscarriage. I had an abortion at Planned Parenthood, and they tied my tubes. I would not bring another child of yours into the world, God forgive me."

Stunned, Sam grabbed his chest. He heaved trying to breathe. Sweat poured down his face. "Jesus save me."

Rita pointed a bony finger at him, jabbing the air like she was stabbing him.

"I packed a bag for you. Take it and go."

Sam staggered outside, his body seeming to melt like watery ice in the summer sun.

He stumbled to his car. He drove up Broad Street to Washington Avenue. He turned left to tenth Street. He drove past the Triangle Tavern,

Pat's Steaks, Geno's Steaks, the Villa D'Roma restaurant, Ralph's, and the outdoor vegetables and fruit stands now manned by Vietnamese merchants. Their chattering sounded like the movie voices of Aliens from Mars.

Sam staggered like a punch-drunk fighter being pummeled from the ropes to the ropes. He was lost, bewildered in his world. A South Philly boy was now a stranger in a strange land he used to call his turf, his home.

I have gone to hell without dying. Maybe I was always dead.

He cradled his gun for a long moment. The full moon took on the smile of a Jack o Lantern. He felt like a fool, like Pagliacci a crying clown, heartbroken, defeated.

He placed the gun in his mouth. The old Dean Martin song flashed across his mind.

"When the moon hits your eye like a big Pizza pie, that's amore."

"Mother of God," he said.

He ended his life not with a whimper and a "Bang."

Hoity Toity

Pedaling, pedaling faster, pedaling under a blanket of sweat, on her early morning Peloton, Isabel Hathaway's body gleamed under the rising summer sun over the Eastern window of her penthouse condo on Rittenhouse Square. Trim at thirty-two, Isabel prided herself on her sleek body. Her black hair was swept into a ponytail. Her workout charged her mind to a decision she had been contemplating for months and had acted on a month ago. She was going to have a child despite her husband Edgar's unfortunate low sperm count.

Edgar needed an heir for his vast fortune handed down from his ancestors who mined coal in north- eastern Pennsylvania. The mines were now toxic pits, smoldering, spewing carbon monoxide into the air around Ashland and other towns long abandoned.

Edgar opened fracking mines claiming these mines used cleaner, greener technology to extract energy from shale. He managed the Hathaway Foundation, a charitable organization founded by his father. The main beneficiary of the Foundation was Philabundance, a highly respected program dedicated to relieving hunger.

They lived well, wanting for nothing, traveling the world, chauffeur driven to concerts and to the Met in New York City for operas. Italian operas only. German operas were too long for Edgar.

Edgar had political ambitions. At forty-four, he looked virile, Hollywood handsome in everything he wore from gym shorts and Tee-shirts to black ties and tuxedos. He felt he was destined to lead.

Isabel loved Edgar, loved their lifestyle, appreciated his Liberal views in a Sanctuary City, his distaste for Trump and adoration of Obama. Tonight, he was to be honored by Philabundance at a donor appreciation dinner.

The sun blazed over the tall trees of the Square. People scurried along the paths below like ants chasing crumbs of food.

The Peloton video pushed her workout. "Faster, faster, faster."

She pressed on, determined to complete her session in record time. Four minutes later, she finished, proud of her new record. Nearly breathless, she toweled the sweat from her lithe body and headed to her private shower. She slept separately from Edgar, though they enjoyed sex at least once a week.

She savored the warm water, soothing and cleansing. She dressed in blue shorts and a loose-fitting yellow top, her favorite colors, sandals, without socks, for now. Her maid Martha, a black woman in her early fifties, with graying hair, dark plastic frames covering sharp black eyes and perpetual smile was never seen by Isabel without apron. Martha had never seen Isabel with an apron.

"Good morning Martha. How about whipping me up a pepper and tomato omelet, whole wheat toast, and a Jamaican blend cup of coffee."

"Certainly, Mrs. Hathaway. Shall I add an avocado on the side?"

"There's a thought. How about avocado toast."

"Yes Ma'am."

Edgar appeared dressed in golf attire. Scotch plaid knickers, Ralph Lauren polo shirt and a plaid tam.

"Good morning, my Emma Stone lookalike."

They smooched playfully.

"What may I prepare for you, Mr. Hathaway?" asked Martha.

"Nothing. I am brunching with Chad Wilson at Merion."

"Dear. Did you forget you are being honored tonight?"

"I shall be home in plenty of time for the festivities at The Prime."

"Not too much drinking."

"One bloody Mary before golf helps my putting. One more after golf helps me forget any bad shots. Besides, I have no intent in letting a scion of the Wilson's beat a Hathaway. He'll be spanked properly. The man can drive a golf ball three hundred yards, but putts with the dexterity of a three-fingered butcher."

Isabel laughed aloud. "You are a smug but adorable scoundrel."

His iPhone X buzzed. "Ah. My Uber driver is downstairs. I am off. Wish your hubby luck. I intend to return as a champion."

"Break a leg my hero."

"Yes. I will kick a butt, too."

He leaned over, pecking her on her cheek. "Look like a movie star tonight."

"Don't I always?"

"Now who is the smug one. Ciao!"

"Good day, Mr. Hathaway," replied Martha.

He did not reply.

Isabel watched him go. She was proud to be his wife. She could not wait to tell him her news.

After breakfast, she called Jessica Smythe Cody, her best friend since her undergraduate days at Swarthmore.

"Hello Jessie."

"Isabel from Hell! How is my BFF?"

"Living the dream. What is new in your world?"

"You will not believe this. Natalie Smedley is getting married to a guy named Carpenter?"

"Is that his name or his profession?" asked Isabel.

"Both. Too damn funny, I'd say. It reminded me of the time when David Butler asked you on a date. You said, you could never marry a man named baker or butler or carpenter or hunter or fisher or archer or anyone whose name bespoke the tradesmen."

"Yes, I remember. But you forgot cooper, gardener and mason."

"Hah. Too true and funny. My hubby owns ten Papa John stores. I call him the King of Pizza and I am his Queen."

"Aren't we the lucky ones," said Isabel.

"I read in Sunday's Inquirer that Edgar is getting an award as outstanding Liberal of Philly. Quite the *hoity toity*, is your husband."

Isabel was tempted to share her news with Jessica, but not until she spoke to Edgar, lest he feel slighted.

She dreaded ever displeasing him.

"Let's do lunch today," said Isabel. "We can do Devin's. My treat."

"Sorry but my nanny is away, so I must do the Mommy thing today."

"Children do restrict one's life."

"Yes. They are worth it."

Isabel sighed. "I suppose so. Will I see you soon?"

"Next week when the nanny returns. I will take the train and walk over to Devin's."

"Wednesday at two, after the lunch crowd goes back to work. We can have any table we want. My treat. I may have some exciting news for you."

"I like excitement. I get damn little as a mommy, or should I say, as a mummy?"

"You would not look fashionable in permanent body wrap."

"Ciao, Isabel."

"Adieu to you."

Isabel peered out the window overlooking the Square. The people coursing the Park looked tiny, like ants scurrying for food.

Located in Ardmore, PA just outside Philly, Merion Golf Club is one of the most exclusive Country Clubs in America. Merion hosted five US Open tournaments. The Club was the course where Legends were made. Bobby Jones completed his Grand slam there. Ben Hogan won the US Open there after recovering from a near fatal car accident. Lee Trevino beat the great Jack Nicklaus to win the US Open in 1960. The course is not long. Nicklaus declared Merion the "best course in the country."

Red baskets adorn the top of each flagpole. Legend states that the signature baskets were the idea of course designer Hugh Irvine Wilson who saw shepherds using baskets to keep their lunch safe from predatory crows and hawks.

On his twenty first birthday, Edgar's father paid Edgar's entry fee. He considered his membership to be an inheritance, a recurring testament of his father's approval and an affirmation of his self-worth. His Dad was a renowned heart surgeon and served on the Board of Directors of two hospitals and several civic organizations. When Dad bestowed the gift of membership, he told Edgar that he must "never forget his pedigree."

Edgar took that advice as a solemn duty. The Hathaways were societal royalty. Reputation and status were paramount. No scandals allowed.

Edgar only associated with members who were second generation or greater. Chad was a "nouveau riche." A graduate of Drexel, Chad was a strong man but dull, not witty or clever. His brute strength had carried him to the finals of the A flight. Edgar was a heavy favorite.

They teed off. The match was on.

Four hours later, Chad and Edgar were deadlocked. Both men were on the 18th green in two.

Chad had a downhill, forty-foot putt. A one in a hundred chance. Edgar had a relatively straight forward, up-hill putt. Victory seemed assured.

Chad eyed the putt and whacked it hard, too hard thought Edgar. The ball sped across the green, racing through three breaks. If it missed the cup, it was off the green and the match was over. The ball raced on, turning sharply left and dropped into the cup.

"Yes!" shouted Chad as loud as an Eagles fan on steroids.

Edgar could save a tie by making his easy putt. He guided the ball up the green. It stopped three inches short, giving Chad his first win ever over Edgar.

"Never up means never in. You can have the rest of that," said Chad.

Edgar tapped his putt in. Chad stood next to him, grinning like a jack-o-lantern.

"Lucky me! Good luck always beats careful planning. Let's have a beer."

Edgar shook Chad's hand feeling like the golf gods had robbed him. He knew from experience golf was often a game of chance.

He walked to the Men's Grille behind Chad. Edgar's stomach twisted in anger; his spirits lower than a water well. His father had taught him–"Win with humility. Lose with honor, like a gentleman."

Word of Chad's win spread cross the clubhouse. Chad repeated that Edgar's putt to tie was short and weak.

Chad laughingly pointed at Edgar. "Edgar never could get it to the hole. Never up, never in."

The allusion to his being childless stung like a wasp sting. He smiled, shrugging his shoulders to deflect the insult.

"He better use his putter better at home or Isabel will find a new golf partner," said Chad.

Edgar fumed from his gut like a man on fire. He resisted the urge to drive a punch into Chad's face. He had heard snide remarks about his lack of children, but suggesting that Isabel would leave him was a low blow.

"Neanderthals are a class above your family," said Edgar.

"At least we have a family," said Chad.

The bar turned deathly silent. Chad stared defiantly at Edgar.

Edgar forced a laugh to deflect the innuendos.

"Hatching is in season for reptiles," he said.

Chad moved towards him; fists curled. "Take that back."

"Retry your putt on 18. I will bet you one thousand to your ten dollars you do not make it."

"Screw you, wimpy dick."

Edgar folded his arms across his chest. "Do not get in a battle of wits, Chad. You are an unarmed man."

The bar exploded in laughter. Chad's complexion burned red. "Let's go outside."

"Go to hell."

Edgar sat motionless. The Pro had witnessed the scene. "That is enough Chad. You are flagged for today."

Insult to injury was a sour dish to eat. Chad had made Edgar an enemy for life.

Chad nodded to the Pro. "Thanks."

He'd tasted defeat and embarrassment on hallowed ground in front of his Club members. Time to call Uber and go home.

The Uber driver was an elderly white man named George. His ruddy complexion spoke of a man who earned his keep by working outside. His sparkling blue eyes and sprinkle of freckles suggested an Irish heritage.

"How was your game Laddie?" asked George.

"I lost my championship to a man who putts like a blacksmith but makes a forty-footer tracking at racehorse speed on the 18th."

“Ouch! You need a taste of Tullamore Dew to soothe your pain. Did you lose to a good man?”

“I need a double Manhattan on the rocks. I lost to a bloody ass hole who is dumber than a tree stump.”

“Hah! A Manhattan is a good choice for a young man like you. Have you got family?"

“Just my wife and I.”

“Children. You need a son to teach and a daughter to protect. Family makes you a man.”

Edgar took a deep breath to control his beating heart. He needed a lecture like he needed a kick in the shins.

Edgar texted Isabel. “I lost. A double Manhattan on the rocks will help.”

She texted back. "Oh no. Your drink will be ready. You have a big night in front of you. And you are still and always will be my winner."

Edgar eased back in his seat. She deserved a better man.

Isabel greeted him with a freshly made Manhattan. She had poured herself a white wine, Riesling. "Hello my dear. Your quaff is ready.”

Edgar pecked her cheek. “Lady Isabel is the queen of queens.”

They sat on the outdoor veranda overlooking Rittenhouse Square. The noise of the street, honking horns, whistles, shouts floated up to their level. The City was alive, calling all to life with the sounds of the late afternoon. The north side of the Square was filled with vegetable stands. The south side along Locust Street bore the tents of would-be artists and antique dealers. The Center was flush with couples on benches. Several homeless people manned benches like a tenant farmer staking his claim to God’s little acre.

“You should have a grand dinner tonight. I love the aura and food at the Prime. Very Hoity Toity,” she said.

Edgar stood by the railing, gazing at the Park, his shoulders slumped. “I am tired. I feel like a failure. I cannot give you a child. One little lean forward and I would join the masses below. My life would end not with a bang but a splat. Tempting.”

Isabel shot up.

"Do not say that. You are a good man. You support a wonderful Foundation that feeds the homeless and poor. You are a savior not a sinner. You represent the best part of Philadelphia. I love you, Edgar."

"I saw myself today for the first time. I am a manufactured man, reared like a pedigree dog to prance at shows. I have wealth but no accomplishments. I am not *hoity toity*. I am as Shakespeare said, a rogue and peasant slave."

Isabel clutched his arm. She pierced his eyes with hers, beaming like lasers from her core. "Listen Dearest Edgar. I have news for you. A miracle has happened far greater than a stupid putt by a stupid man or any derision by ignorant fools."

"How so?"

She cupped his face in her hands. "I am carrying your child."

Edgar gasped. "What? That is impossible."

She caressed his cheek, like a mother comforting her worried child. "It is as true as my love for you."

Edgar feared she had cheated on him. His insecurity sent his mind in a tailspin. "Isabel. What have you done?"

"You cannot believe I cheated on you. I have not had sex with another man since the moment I met you. I swear on the soul of my mother."

Edgar stared wild-eyed at her, disbelief and joy dripping from his eyes. "Dear Sweet Jesus. What god wrought this miracle?"

Isabel clasped him to her bosom like a mother holds a child. "You are a great man Edgar Hathaway. You are going to be a greater father."

Edgar had never cried in his adult life. Tears washed his face as the sun surrounded Isabel in a glow. "Thank you, Isabel. I shall be the best father ever. Better than my father. My God, I am Hoity Toity lucky!"

"You need a shower, Dearest. May I join you?"

Edgar pulled her against his chest. "I am so damn lucky."

Later, Edgar left for the dinner, smiling, self-assured, happy. Isabel watched him stride across the Square like a man who owned his City. He waved to her, shooting a thumbs up. She blew a kiss.

Her eyes misted in satisfaction. She had saved Edgar. He would never know she had in vitro conception.

The sperm was carefully selected from a Scandinavian man. Hopefully, the child would be healthy and look like Edgar. Whitman had written, "The child is the father of the man." Different context. True in Edgar's case, she thought.

She caught sight of Billy Penn's statue atop City Hall. Penn came here to avoid religious persecution. He created a great City wherein a great country was born. Isabel created a new world for she and Edgar.

She patted her stomach. No one would ever know how and why she had wrought this miracle of childbirth. It was a fitting accomplishment. The child would save its father and her as well.

“God bless the Child.”

Mummers and Strummers

Two Streeters are inhabitants of the two-story brick and stone row houses on Second Street near Washington Avenue. The people are generational performers in the annual Mummers day parade, a multi- century Philadelphia tradition. The parade has a checkered history of charges of racism, sexism and homophobia sprinkled through its comic section, string bands and fancy brigades. The Two Streeters deny the claims. Their counter to all claims of social impropriety is their position that they are costumed dancers and parade for the pure enjoyment of their families, friends and the City. They make their own costumes and floats and bring the City together. If you cannot take a joke, move to the suburbs and sip white wine on the rocks with your little finger raised.

On September 11, 2001 at 9:10 AM, Stefan Jurgenson entered the world in the usual way. While terrorists flew planes into the World Trade Center, Stefan continued the Jurgenson family line, crying. His father Kurt and mother Elsa later felt that his timing signified Stefan as a special child sent by God so they could rejoice while the rest of America remembered, reflected and swore to avenge the terroristic attacks.

Stefan was eight years old when his father took him to the Mummers Museum. They walked among the displays of costumes and floats from past parades until Kurt stopped in front of a dancer in a comic outfit, his face smeared in black.

"That is your Grandfather Sven's costume. He was a legend among Two Streeters. He could out drink any man, out fight and out dance any Mummer. He played the banjo with a passion. No man played Golden Slippers like my father."

Stefan squeezed his Dad's hand in disbelief. "Grand Pop was white with silver hair. This man is black."

Kurt laughed heartily. "You sound like a flaming liberal. It is a show my son, a minstrel show at that. Old Sven did not have a bone of prejudice in his body."

Stefan did not like that what he saw was not what he was being told, a trait that he held in his heart and mind as surely as if God implanted it into his DNA.

That night, a vision of Grandfather's black face seared his sleeping mind. He awoke screaming for his Mother. Kurt clasped the hysterical child in his strong ironworker arms. "Stefan, my son. Your Father and mother are here. What frightened you?"

Stefan sprung from his father into Elsa's arms. "I saw Grandfather Sven as a Negro man coming to get me."

"Your grandfather is in his grave, my boy," said Kurt.

Elsa rocked him from side to side. "We are here Stefan. We are here. No one will harm you."

"He will sleep with me tonight," said Elsa.

"As you wish," said Kurt.

Elsa carried Stefan to the master bedroom. She wrapped him in the sheets and bedspread. Pregnant five and a half, months, she did not want or need lovemaking tonight and the boy needed his mother.

Kurt took Stefan's bed. In a few moments, he snored the doors off their hinges.

Stefan snuggled next to his mother. "Are black people evil?"

"Their evil is no worse than the evil devils in white men. Pray the Lord's prayer with me. No devil dare come to you when you pray to God."

They prayed the Our Father three times before Stefan fell asleep. He prayed every night at bedtime for six years.

Three and a half months later, Gerald Jurgenson was born on New Year's Day at noon. Kurt missed the birth. He was marching in the Mummers parade strumming his father's banjo, Stefan at his side, an unwilling participant. The banjo played on as a dancing Kurt smiled to the crowd lining the sidewalk. He sang aloud. "O those golden slippers. O those golden slippers."

Stefan held his hands over his ears, fearing the man in the black face would hear the song and want to join the parade.

The day had started at six AM with all members gathered at Second Street in full costume. Stefan had begged Kurt to let him go the hospital with his mother. Kurt reprimanded him for "Not upholding family tradition."

The Two Streeters warmed themselves with hot coffee laced with Jamison Irish whiskey.

"Tis the breakfast of Champions" hailed Kurt, in a nasally brogue worthy of a bad ventriloquist, or at least a drunk one. The smell of the whiskey repelled Stefan, sick to his stomach with worry about his mother. What if Grandpop's ghost visited her room and scared her?

The band tuned their banjos in a cacophony resembling the squeal of tires swirling along Two Street.

His father looked like a stranger under his red clown mask. Stefan looked for a way to escape the madness. Kurt eyed him, as if reading his mind. Stefan wanted to scream or cry or just run away.

They marched to the staging area. The crowds were forming. Beach chairs, folding chairs and small wagons lined the sidewalks. Partying had begun. Whiskey bottles and beer cans flashed in the morning sun. The band members huddled in groups of three or four, laughing in the frigid morning air. Getting drunk was a good way to stay warm.

Their smiles and bouts of laughter astonished Stefan. Did they not know it was freezing? Did they not care his mother was in the hospital?

It was ten AM now and cold, drizzly rain splattered the marchers. Stefan feared his half-drunk father would slip and break his leg while he did his Mummer's strut dance.

The crowd cheered Kurt. Why is he a hero?

After the parade, Kurt took Stefan to Elsa's hospital room. She was sitting up in her bed, her dirty blond hair pulled back. He exhaled and ran to her side. "Mama. Mama. Are you okay?"

"Say hello to your brother Gerald."

Stefan peered at the tiny figure, resting on Mama's chest. eyes closed.

"Is he not beautiful?" she said.

"You are beautiful mother. He is all red and wrinkled."

Stefan scored well on all his report cards and aced all his tests. His academic prowess landed him a spot at Central High School, the premier school of Philly. His academic achievements continued at Central. In his senior year, he expected to win a National Merit Scholarship and attend Penn. Leaving Philly was out of the question.

His father insisted he attend the parade in honor of his family tradition. He did so grudgingly.

On his birthday in 2019, Elsa cooked him a round roast dinner. She baked a vanilla cake, topped with chocolate icing.

The family finished dinner, lit birthday candles and all sang "Happy Birthday."

Kurt brought out a large box, wrapped in birthday paper.

"This is for you, Son. You are eighteen and a man. You need to carry on the family tradition. We Swedes and the Finns started the Mummers Day parades. The shanty Irish and Dagos and black people and Wetbacks came later."

Stefan cringed at the racial epithets. His best friends at Central were a blend of all races, religions and ethnic backgrounds. His best friend was a Jewish boy from West Oak Lane whose father was a doctor. He unwrapped the gift slowly until his hands rested on the banjo strings.

"Is this Grandpop's banjo?"

Kurt flashed a smile, his light blue eyes beaming like the crystal chandelier over the dining room table.

"No. It is now yours to carry on the next Mummer's day parade. Do you hear me Stefan? You are the new standard bearer of the Jurgenson family. Be proud, Son. Be proud."

Stefan pulled his hands away. "I cannot accept this gift."

Kurt's cheeks burned under his furrowed brow and narrow eyes. "How dare you reject my gift? How dare you insult me and my family?"

Kurt loomed over Stefan. He slapped Stefan hard across his cheeks. "Damn schools teach children to disrespect their parents."

Elsa jumped to Stefan's side. "Are you hurt, Stefan?"

"No mother. I am fine."

Stefan eased his mother aside. “Would it surprise you that the song "O dem golden slippers" was composed by a black man named James Bland in 1879? Bland also played the banjo. The Mummers are not solely a white parade based on Swedish traditions. It is rooted in a tradition of diversity. Think about that Father.”

“The Mummers have allowed black marchers and clubs. We are not racists. Black face is part of the minstrel origins. We honor those origins.”

“How many members of your band are black or Hispanic or Asian?”

“None.”

“Expand your mind Dad. Include all people, not just the ones you allow. Beat me if you will, but I will not march unless one of my black friends parades with me.”

Kurt thrust his chin out. “Find one that can play a banjo and he can parade with you and me.”

“Do you mean that?”

“Yes. I struck you because you rejected my gift. Take it and walk beside me. Bring a black friend.”

Stefan finished unwrapping the banjo. He handed it to Kurt. “Teach me how to play this instrument.”

Kurt held his chin up. "You stood up to me and took the hit like a man. I can respect you. Can you respect our traditions?"

“Yes, if they match the times. If they represent decency and include all in the great parade of life we are all marching.”

Kurt started playing, “O dem golden slippers.”

Gerald danced the Mummers strut around the dining room. “I want to march too,” he said.

“Me too,” said Elsa.

“We will march as a family,” said Stefan. He was not including his grandfather’s ghost in his invitation.

Food Fight in Philly

Every City has a food that symbolizes its culture. Chicago has deep dish pizza. New York, cheesecake. Boston, baked beans. New Orleans, Creole. Miami, Cuban pork sandwiches. And Philly, cheesesteaks.

The one question all visitors ask of Philly folk– *Where do I get the best cheesesteak*?

Philly food magazine, *Mangia*, decided to run a contest inviting a premier list of the City's better-known cheesesteak shops. John's Pulled Pork, Dalessandro's, Barry's, Steve's, Pat's, Geno's, Prince of Steaks, Jim's, and Mama's headed the All-Star list. Entry fee was ten thousand each, winner take all.

The contest got wide media attention and made national news.

A blue-ribbon panel of three Philly based chefs was authorized to make the call.

Philly had held Wing Bowl, a contest to see who could eat the most wings. The Venue was Wells Fargo Center, home of the Sixers and Flyers. It always sold out. But this was a food joust for the ages and the pride of the City.

Emilio Pasquale read the story while sitting on his front steps on Federal Street near Seventh Street. Emilio owned a corner eatery and food store on Seventh Street, a legacy from his father Arturo, and mother Concetta now resting in God's arms.

His white, sleeveless tee shirt clung to his hairy chest on his five-foot six-inch, wiry frame. He wore faded grey, low-cut walking shoes, stuffed with Doctor Scholl's insoles. His arches had fallen ten years ago.

It was late August, the week before Labor Day. The humidity and heat withered the city in a breathless oven.

Emilio, called out to his wife Lucia, "Come talk to me. I need to show you something important."

Lucia did not answer immediately. He called out again. No answer. He went inside and found her sitting in her recliner, her hefty legs jutting along the raised recliner, a fan blowing hard on her pretty face, and salt and pepper hair swept high off her sweaty brow. She was watching Jeopardy, her favorite show. No one could get her away from the show. The carpets were worn as were the curtains on the front window. A blanket covered the upholstered brown sofa. The cherry wood coffee table held a plastic tray and a pitcher of iced tea laced with mint leaves and lemons. Lucia was settled in for the evening.

"Why didn't you answer me when I called for you?" he asked.

"You asked me to come outside. Only a fool would leave the fan for the heat."

He grunted and handed her the *Mangia* article. "Look at this article. *Mangia Magazine* is holding a contest to see who makes the best cheesesteak in Philly. It costs ten grand to compete. Winner take all. I can win that contest."

"You been in the sun too long. Your freaking brain is fried. It is a stunt. The big shots will get thousands of dollars of free publicity. The winnings are chump change to them. And what makes you think you can win it? And where are you going to get ten thousand dollars to enter the contest? Don't be a Calabrese Capo Dos hard head. Go watch the Phillies, forget about this contest and get a good night's sleep. There is melatonin in the bathroom cabinet."

Emilio fumed at her logic. She was smarter than him. But he could cook. He knew cheesesteaks. "I have a plan to win it."

Lucia sighed, as though she was raising an incorrigible child. "God spare me."

Emilio had no plan, yet. He had been a poker player all his life. He could smell a big pot brewing before the cards had been dealt.

He went upstairs, washed up in the sink, sprayed cologne, changed into jeans and a clean black polo shirt. He had a thirty-four-inch waist and forty-four shoulders. His top gleamed like a cue ball. The kids used to call him Daddy Popeye. They sang, “He’s Popeye the cheesesteak man. Strong to the finish, he makes me eat spinach. He’s Popeye the cheesesteak man.”

Emilio strode down Federal Street and called Uber for a ride to the Sugar House Casino.

The Casino offered relief from the heat and a chance to play two dollar no limit hold ‘em.

The pit boss found him a table ahead of seven others waiting in line. Regulars rate.

He played for an hour, breaking even by playing tight. Then a crazy young guy with tattoos up both arms and around his neck put him all in. Emilio could not afford the loss. He folded. The kid laughed and showed him the seven deuce off suit, the worst hand in poker.

“Nice hand,” said Emilio.

He played through his big blind and left, offering the kid a "thumbs up."

“You got balls, Junior.”

The tattooed man smirked. "Just two, like you."

Emilio took an Uber home. Lucia was asleep on her easy chair, snoring like a drunk. He stood over her, careful not to disturb her. She looked pretty, despite the wheezing and heavy arms and legs. He loved her.

The *Mangia* article in hand, Emilio crawled into bed, exhausted but restless. All cheesesteaks are made with the same ingredients. Younger cooks use bacon to grease the skillet or frying plate. All use quality rib eye, provolone or Cheese Whiz, onions, pepper, salt. They use the same fryers. The bread may vary, but it is always freshly delivered daily. How could he make his cheesesteak stand out? If only he had a secret ingredient, a certain pepper or spice or what?

The article was written by a guy named Alexander Pierce. A *Metagon* for sure. Probably a Penn or Princeton Graduate. The kind of guy who thinks he knows everything. The kind of guy who is dealt a pat hand in life, for life.

Emilio had salted away fifteen thousand Lucia did not know about.

One of the benefits of running a mostly cash business. He lapsed into a nervous sleep, tossing and turning until the sun awoke him. The morning sun crept around the edges of his Venetian blinds. The aroma of fresh brewed coffee from the kitchen signaled Lucia had risen. He tiptoed to the bathroom. He needed a shave and shower before he saw her questioning visage. The warm water washed away the sweat from his body. He dried himself, looking at the man in the mirror, an aging man who folded to seven-deuce the night before. The bedside clock read seven-o-two. Ironic. He slipped on fresh Jockey underwear, jeans, a Phillies tee shirt, white socks, and low-cut sneakers. The clock had stopped at seven-o-two. His mind rattled like an alarm clock. The secret ingredient shot like a bolt of lightning in his mind, an epiphany. He had the key to win. His heart jumped like a kangaroo in heat.

"Yes!"

He would call on Alex Pierce today. The food fight was on.

Alex was a tall, willowy man. He wore black-rimmed designer glasses over his pale blue eyes. His sandy hair, parted on the right side, combed neatly like a schoolboy.

His office was a two-story walk up unit on Third Street in Society Hill off Head House Square, fitting the motif of a preppy trying to be fashionably independent.

Diplomas from Penn for a BA and an MBA from Wharton hung like twins on the wall behind his desk.

"Your call intrigued me," said Alex. "I like mysteries. What is this secret ingredient you have discovered that makes your cheesesteaks better than all others in Philadelphia?"

"If I tell you, it will not be a secret," said Emilio. "Let's just say that it is the family recipe handed down to me from my grandfather."

Alex's brow furrowed into wrinkles of disbelief. "You would have me believe that you have developed the best cheesesteak in Philly over the litany of cheesesteak legends we have assembled?"

Emilio pulled a thick envelope from his jeans and laid it on Alex's desk. "Here is ten grand to back up my claim. I am putting my money where my mouth is. Count me in on the competition."

Alex opened the envelope. "I prefer a check."

"No check. Just write me a receipt and put the word out that Emilio Pasquale has entered his chef's hat into the ring with a secret that will win him the prize."

"Is this for real or a publicity stunt?"

"Hey. Does the cash look real? Are you afraid I can beat the big boys? Just say that the Rocky Balboa of cheesesteaks is in for the title."

Alex laughed. "I like that line. It makes for a good story."

Emilio offered a hand. "Then it is a deal?"

Alex clasped Emilio's hand hard, shaking his arm up and down. "We have a deal. I will send out a Press Release that Emilio is in. What is the name of your shop?"

"As of today, it is called The Secret Cheesesteak Shop. Philly's Finest, located on Seventh Street just below Federal."

Emilio walked away, whistling like a schoolboy who beat getting caught by a nun for sneaking out of class early. His next stop was to see Harry Gershman, owner of the Not So Famous Deli and a major bookie. Harry was an old friend. He welcomed Emilio into his back room. Harry bulked out at three hundred pounds, with a belly bigger than a blimp. His jowls shook as he talked.

"What can I do for my Italian Stallion?" asked Harry.

Emilio told him about the contest. "I want you to set up a line on the Street about who will win the contest. I figure I have to be a hundred to one long shot."

Harry chuckled. "Maybe more. I will treat it like a horse race and handicap the entrants. You will be the long shot. What makes you think you can win?"

"I have a secret ingredient that none of the others offer. Let word leak that Emilio has this secret passed down from his ancestors. It is a Calabrese secret."

Harry wagged a ham hock fist in the air. "You have chutzpah. Okay. We can have a ton of fun. I hope your secret sauce is a winner."

"It will win," said Emilio.

Emilio walked away from Harry, happy. His next move was to contact the local radio sports stations. Philly had celebrated Wing Bowl for twenty years. Fans poured into the Wells Fargo Center to watch a chicken wing eating contest. He called the stations to hype the "Steak Out," adding there was a Rocky-like contender who had a secret ingredient. The DJ's lapped up the underdog role of Emilio's steaks.

Business soared as curious Philadelphians flocked to his shop. They left raving about the steaks. Emilio had his ten-grand back in three weeks. His dream of winning the contest haunted him. Lucia picked up on his success.

A week before the contest, she told him over dinner, "You crazy bastard. You better win. Tell me. What is the secret?"

Emilio put a finger to his lips. "Loose lips sink ships."

"I am your wife, not some Nazi spy. What the hell did you put in the sandwiches?"

Emilio refused to tell her.

Alex added to the hype when Emilio told him quietly that bookies had moved the odds on him winning from a thousand to one to fifty to one.

Talk radio stirred the pot like it was homemade gravy. Harry booked more bets on the contest than he normally took on an Eagles game day. Emilio was now the favorite at even money.

They announced the Street odds with a rendition of the Rocky theme song. Emilio loved the hype but had no plans of running up the seventy-two steps of the Philadelphia Art Museum.

Two nights before the contest, Alex had all contestants and Judges meet at the legendary Villa di Roma restaurant on Ninth Street for a pasta dinner and a discussion of the rules. Emilio was introduced in turn. He got a cold reception. A local TV reporter named Cheryl slipped a microphone to his face.

"Emilio. Why will you win?"

Emilio caught the eye of each judge. "Because I have the best Cheesesteak in all of Philly. The whole City knows it. My competitors know it.

When the Judges taste my steak, they will enjoy the secrets of my ancestors. I am blessed with an ingredient sent from God!"

"Wow!" she exclaimed.

The Judges looked at each other like people caught in a storm with no life jackets.

Alex tapped his spoon against his wine glass. "I have given considerable thought regarding the best way to ensure fairness in the judging process. Here are the new rules."

Emilio's heart skipped a beat. His plan had been going so well. Any change could be harmful.

Alex read from his iPhone. "I am sending each of you an email spelling out the rules. Tonight, each of you nine will select a slip of paper with a number on it. It is three part. Tear off one and keep it in your wallet. That will be your identifier. Keep the other two slips. When you return tomorrow at six PM, you will each make your cheesesteak and cut it in halves. Place one slip inside each half of the wrapper of your cheesesteak. The Judges will taste all nine and set aside the one they like best. We will look inside and count the selections. The Cheesesteak with the most votes wins. If there is a tie, the Judges will taste the second half and vote. Whoever gets the most votes wins. This way the Judges will not be influenced by any elements outside their taste buds. Any questions?"

"Very fair," said one contestant.

Emilio felt like the Penn Grad had just kicked him below the belt. Then he recovered, realizing that He had drawn number three. His lucky number. He and Lucia were both born on the third of the month. He was born in August and she was born ten months later, on June third.

He thanked Alex for dinner and called Uber.

Emilio found Lucia amazingly awake. She turned off the television. "How did it go?"

He sat on the sofa in a heap. "I lost my edge."

"They found out your secret ingredient?"

"There is no secret ingredient. I was running a seven-deuce bluff on the

Judges. That smart ass Alex snookered me. He took away the intimidation factor. I figured if I put enough pressure on the Judges, they had to vote for me. It damn near worked."

"So now you have to play the game on the square."

"Bluffing is part of the game."

Lucia cupped his face in her hands. "Don't worry. Just get up tomorrow and make the best freaking Cheesesteak in Philly history."

"I will try," he said, downcast, resigned.

Lucia lifted his chin. "Emilio. You have been more alive in the past month than the past ten years."

She took his hand. "Come with me, my man. I will make sure you get a good night's sleep."

"Your wish is my command."

Three newspaper reporters, a TV camera man and a TV reporter clustered on his steps. He carried the makings of his cheesesteak in a refrigerated bag.

"Emilio. Good luck. How confident are you that you will win?" asked a reporter.

"My secret will carry me through."

"Will you reveal the secret once the contest is over?"

Emilio sped towards the Uber. "Does Coke tell Pepsi its formula?"

"Go get them Rocky!" exclaimed the TV Reporter.

It took only five minutes each to cook the cheesesteaks. Emilio handed his in and headed to the bar badly in need of a glass of wine. Alex approached. "Good luck, Emilio. You know if you win, the secret you hold is worth a fortune."

Emilio sighed. "We shall see."

Alex went to the Judges. "We have tallied the vote. Two contestants received two votes. They are numbers six and three. We will now have the Judges do a test. Best two of three wins."

Emilio barely contained his surprise. The gods of cheesesteaks had looked down on him. He texted Lucia. "Your loving brought me luck. I am head to head to win it all."

Would seven deuce hold up?

Five minutes later, Alex returned. Cameras began to flash. TV tape rolled. "I want to thank all participants in what may become an annual event. The final tally is a two to one vote in favor of John's. Congratulations to John's. The Best Cheesesteak won. And congratulations to Philly's Rocky for a great food fight."

Emilio raised his arms. "Rocky lost a split decision. He later won the championship. I will be back next year and best of luck with my secret."

Emilio and the other contestants exchanged pleasantries. Emilio wanted to run up the Art Museum steps but thought better of it. Cheesesteaks are not great health food. But they are great Philly food. He felt like a winner.

"Mangia, Philadelphia."

Law and Disorder

In her twenty-fourth year of marriage to Fourteenth District Police Captain Mason Hart, Karen Simpson Hart judged his wake-up mood by the way he descended the stairs in their two-story, West Mount Airy home. Today was the second day in a row he thumped down the steps heavy-footed, meaning he was in a sour mood. He had good reason. His life-long friend Chuck Faraday had been shot by a drive-by shooter while sitting in his unmarked car on Germantown Avenue. The shooter opened fire on Chuck and his partner Lester Miles while they drank coffee seated in their car in front of a Starbucks in Chestnut Hill. Lester got lucky. No bullets hit him. Chuck caught one to his head. He was in critical condition in Penn Presbyterian Hospital.

"Morning Karen," said Mason.

"Hi Hon. How is Chuck? Sit. I will bring you coffee. I made Mama Simpson's oatmeal."

Mason dropped into a round-back wooden chair at the head of the oak kitchen table. The Autumn sun greeted him with blinding light from the kitchen window. He moved his chair to one side.

"Chuck is hanging on. Damn shooter laughed as he was firing. Worse, if we find the fool, Old Uncle Barry, our DA, will probably never prosecute the guy, or will offer him a deal."

"That DA is way too liberal, even for me."

Mason pointed his spoon at her. "Someday my dear lady, you will outgrow your liberalism and become a Conservative like me."

"Hah! Black people are not supposed to be Conservatives."

"I am black on the outside, blue on the inside. The oatmeal is good. Your mama taught you well."

Karen handed him the Inquirer. "The Inquirer ran a story speculating that the shooting was not a random act. They say sources told them that

Chuck was mixed up in something to do with opioids. Here. Read it for yourself."

Mason speed read the column and slammed it face down on the table. "Trash! Fake news. Chuck was as straight as Broad Street."

Karen sat and tasted the oatmeal. She preferred fruit and yogurt for breakfast.

She tapped her forefinger on the article. "The reporter asks the question, 'If the officers were in an unmarked car, how did the shooter know they were cops? What were they working on that aroused enough fear in someone to have them shot?'"

Mason knew the answer but dare not tell Karen, as there may be more killing.

"We will find the motive."

Mason's iPhone buzzed a text. He read it and pounded his fist on the table. "Chuck just died."

"Oh no. I am so sorry," said Karen.

"I better go," said Mason, pulling on his uniform jacket.

Karen threw her long, thin arms around him. "Mason, please be careful."

"You go teach your classes. I will handle things on my end."

"I will call the kids," she said. "They loved Uncle Chuckles."

Mason embraced Karen for a long moment. "Two more years and I can retire."

"Mason. Get the bastard who killed Chuck."

"Damn straight I will."

He headed to the District angry and perplexed by the lingering question of how the shooter knew the men in the unmarked car were policemen. He had sent Charles Faraday to an early death.

The Fourteenth District serves as a Magistrate's Court for misdemeanors, DUIs, and holding cells. The Court area was filled with Officers and staff. They milled around the open area; their voices muffled, their heads bowed, the American flag hung behind the Judge's desk, a solemn reminder that police work is a daily war fought in the streets among countrymen.

Standing at the Judge's desk above the crowd, Mason asked for quiet. The murmuring ceased. All eyes were riveted on him. They looked like a church full of penitents awaiting admonishment.

"Chuck Faraday passed away early this morning. He leaves behind a wife, three boys, and us. He was part of our family. We must find his killer. I am personally taking charge of the investigation. The Chief of Police and Mayor of our City expressed their deepest sympathy."

"What about the DA? What have you heard from Uncle Barry?" asked Gary Biggs, a homicide Detective.

"The DA has assigned the case to ADA Kevin Burns."

"Cousin Kevin. That's Uncle Barry's favorite plead out artist. We want the State to get involved," said Biggs. The crowd grumbled their agreement.

Mason held up his hands. "Stay cool people. We have a job to do. We must find the killer. This is no time for playing political games. I want all of you to grab every confidential informant, lift them up by their ankles and shake them until the truth falls out of their mouths, ears, noses, or assholes. Somebody knows something. Am I clear?"

The crowd called out in unison. "Yes!"

"Dismissed."

The police and staff cleared away, except for CSI doctor, Indira Madahar. She held a folder in her hand. Mason nodded to her and motioned her towards his office.

Indira was a brilliant CSI, the most thorough forensics officer Mason knew. She sat across from him, her black eyes glowing like burning charcoal. He admired her brain and feared he was far too attracted to her for his own good.

"I did my analysis of the scene. I tracked the path of the six bullets fired at Chuck. Three hit him. Three others missed and shattered the glass on Miles's side. The only way Miles could not have been hit is if he ducked low. Conclusion, he saw the shooter first or knew the shooter was about to fire. How could he know either event without a pre-event warning of the attack?"

She extracted two pages from the report, showing redlines for the path of each bullet.

"Son of a bitch. Are you sure?"

"Check the lines of fire as calibrated by the computer simulator. Miles has some explaining to do."

"Could Miles have been the target?"

"The lights from the Starbucks store are LEDs. Very bright LEDs. Charles was milk white. Miles was Hershey chocolate brown. Hard to mistake them."

"Thank you, Indira. Please keep this report confidential. If anyone presses you for information, refer them to me."

Indira nodded in agreement. "Where is the investigation leading?"

Mason put the folder in his briefcase. "You will learn soon enough. You have been very helpful."

She rose and stared at him, smiling. "I would do anything for you Captain."

Mason sighed. "I will bear that sentiment in mind."

Mason's private iPhone jingled the Star-Spangled Banner. "I need to take this call."

She turned away, glancing a smile over her shoulder.

He answered the call from Arthur Travis, Pennsylvania State Attorney.

"Hello, Art."

"Hello, Mason. I just got the news about Charles. I am so sorry."

"Thanks. He was a good man and a better policeman. CSI Madahar just left. Based on the pattern and trajectory of the bullets, Miles must have ducked just in time to avoid getting shot. Either he knew about the hit or was the luckiest bastard in America."

"Wow. Who do you think ordered the hit?"

"Chuck Faraday suspected that someone in the DA's office was getting payoffs for reducing the charges against certain drug dealers. He did not suspect Uncle Barry. Old Uncle Barry is a zealot and anti-police, but not a crook. A week ago, Charlie asked my intelligence team to analyze the past two years of case history to see if Uncle Barry had a "nephew" or "niece" with lower scruples and ties to drug dealers. We need to check bank records, too. Charlie probably left a file. Today's Inquirer printed a story that Chuck may have been on the take. It sounds like certain people are closing ranks and sliming Charlie to cover their asses."

"Yes. The rats smell the poison."

Mason met with Bridget Faraday at her home in Roxborough to convey his sympathies and the condolences of the entire police force. Chief of Police Richard Knox had paid his respects in person. Knox was a good leader and honest. Mason held off informing Knox about the case Chuck and he were working, fearful that Knox would tell the Mayor and Uncle Barry about his suspicions. He had no real evidence. Uncle Barry would sweep it under the carpet.

They sat at her kitchen table over coffee. A bottle of Jameson stood on the Formica counter. Mason needed a drink. "Want a shot?" she asked.

He declined her offer.

Bags puffed under her blue-green eyes. She had gained a few pounds, but the weight did not diminish her angelic face.

"I am so sorry Bridget. How are the kids?"

"Linda is upstairs in her room. She refuses to come out. Jerry is at O Malley's pub with his friends and a few cousins. He is shattered. All the Irish whiskey in Philly will not console him. Why did someone kill Chuck?"

Mason took her hand. "What I can tell you in strictest confidence is Chuck was on a special assignment, working a very sensitive case. I fear he may have been getting close to a major arrest. I cannot tell you more. Please, not a word to anyone."

"The Inquirer ran a story suggesting Chuck was on the take. I swear on the eyes of my children, he never took a dime."

"We know Chuck was an honorable man. I will not let that left-wing rag ruin him. For now, please trust me. I will find the truth, so help me Jesus."

Bridget teared up. "Mason. Two weeks ago, a mob in North Philly shot six cops and people threw rocks and bottles at the cops trying to protect them. What is going on in our society?"

"Law and disorder replaced law and order as a way of life. My job is to restore justice and keep the peace. We will do it no matter what forces are arrayed against us."

"I see that. I pray you win."

Mason patted her hand. "We have to win the battle of the Streets, or Philly will become the City of Brotherly Hate."

He called the Desk Sergeant from his iPhone. "Bring in Lester Miles. I want a copy of his report on Chuck's shooting on my desk when I return."

"Call me if you need anything."

"I need justice for Charlie."

"So do I."

Mason read Lester's report twice. Lester described the shooting as a random attack. He called in the attack. He did not get a good look at the shooter except that he was a black man with a toothy smile and hyena laugh, like a crack head higher than Billy Penn's hat.

Lester Miles had a solid record as a policeman. He and Chuck were partners for over three years. Lester had no blemishes on his record.

Lester stood about five foot nine. Trim and athletic, he had boxed golden gloves and served two years in the Army. His light brown shirt matched his complexion.

He shook hands with Mason. The man had a fighter's grip.

"Hello Captain. I am sick about Charles. How can I help you? Have you talked to Bridget? How can I help her?"

Mason sat back; his arms folded across his chest. "I read your report of the shooting. You guys were caught off guard. What were you doing in Chestnut Hill at ten forty-seven?"

"We were working the case."

"What case?"

"The Cousin case. That is what Chuck called it. He said Uncle Barry had a bunch of cousins working for him and he expected to find proof that the DA's office was tied into High Hat Gamble's crew. I did not mention that in my report because Chuck had me sworn to secrecy. He said you demanded that we talk to no one except you about our findings. I kept my word by leaving it out of the report. I just wrote that we were off shift and wanted a cup of Starbucks. Did I do right?"

Mason nodded, rocking in his high-back leather chair. "Yeah. You did right. How does High Hat fit into the scheme of things?"

"Charlie was driving home last week around ten. He usually drives up Lincoln Drive but there was an accident just above Horrter Street, so he turned right on Horrter to go around the jammed traffic. He cut up Pelham to Cresheim Road near Cecilian Academy. He saw High Holmes's yellow Mustang parked off to the side. Another car was parked in front of it facing the opposite way. Chuck could not catch the license plate. He drove down Cresheim Road, did a U'y and came up the street. He photo'd the plate as he rode by."

Mason's heart raced, sensing a breakthrough. "Whose plate is it?"

"Chuck never told me."

"Where is his iPhone? Who ran the plate?"

"The iPhone is probably in the evidence room."

"Why didn't you tell me this sooner?"

"I thought Chuck was going to make it and he should tell you. I never saw the plate report."

"We have the plate number on the iPhone. We can run it."

Mason rolled his eyes, wondering how Lester had lasted fourteen years as a policeman.

"Find High Hat and bring him to me. If he balks, bring him anyway. My old buddy and I need to reconnect."

"High Hat is not going to like being rousted. I best bring back up."

Mason grabbed Lester's collar. "No back up. Just tell High Hat that I want to ask him about his half-brother, Chiclets."

"Who or what is Chiclets?"

"Large white, slabs of bubble gum capsules like the smiling teeth you saw in the shooter's mouth. We nicknamed High Hat's half-brother, Norman Chiclets."

Lester stood up, sighing. "Damn. Why can't I have back-up?"

"Just bring him in. Back-up will draw attention and will force High Hat to make a stand that could get ugly."

"I see your point, Captain."

Mason pointed to the door. "Go."

Mason ordered the Desk Sergeant, Martha Sears, to bring all Chuck's belongings to his office. He could not afford to break the chain of evidence custody, but he needed to open the iPhone right away.

Martha was a fifty-one-year-old veteran Policewoman who oozed character. If Mason were the District boss, she was the district Godmother. Gangly, her salt and pepper hair usually mussed over her droopy, hazel eyes and puffy cheeks, she entered his office with an evidence bag in hand.

"Hello, Martha. Please lay the contents on my desk. Notate what I handle."

"Yes, Captain."

Mason took out the iPhone. He opened the picture roll. It was time stamped and dated. The license plate on the dark blue SUV began with the tell-tale letters "MG"–Municipal Government.

"Please take everything back to the evidence locker. Make sure it is relogged properly. Then run the plate and bring the report to me, immediately. Not a word to anyone."

"Got it Captain."

Mason checked his watch. He could not wait to talk to Moses High Hat Holmes.

High Hat was born on May 31, 1983, the last time the Philadelphia Seventy-Sixers won the NBA title. His mother named him after Seventy-Sixer center, Moses Malone. He earned the nickname 'High Hat' when his gym teacher at Germantown said he looked higher than High Hat ceiling lights.His basketball career ended when a police car ran him down accidentally during a car chase. The police car rammed into his knee, shattering the patella, his dreams of the NBA gone in a flash of bad luck. He limped like a tilting giant.

Moses found a new trade–drugs. His first team was a few kids selling dime bags during Summer League games around the City. His business grew. His legend grew. Word on the street was that High Hat had a new, more sinister meaning. High H.

High Hat's only arrest was by a rookie patrolman–Mason Hart. The charges were dropped. Mason never got over the sickening, dispirited feeling that Moses beat the system. Moses never forgave Mason for tagging him.

High Hat sauntered into Mason's office. "Hello Big Shit, Big Shot," said Moses.

"Hello Moses. You can leave right after you tell me where I can find Chiclets."

Moses smirked. "Amazon has them for sale. Walmart, too."

"Don't play word games with me. Where is your boy, Chiclets?"

"Don't know."

"We know he shot Chuck Faraday. We can prove it. Do you think he is not going to give you up? I want him now or we will close every street corner where you do business until we get him."

Moses loomed over Mason, sneering disdain. "What kind of bull crap are you throwing at me?"

"He shot a cop. A woman and two kids are in mourning. We want him now."

Moses dragged his leg across the office. "I want my knee back. When I get my knee, you get Chiclets."

Moses limped away. Mason shut the door. "Good riddance."

"Put a tail on him. He will ice Chiclets as sure as God made little green apples."

Martha entered carrying a grimace and a report.

"We ran the license plate. It belongs to ADA Kevin Burns."

"Hold on to that information. If we bring him in too soon, the Chief, the Mayor and Uncle Barry will circle the wagons. We need solid proof of conspiracy and bribes. Keep this quiet. That is an order."

His office clear, Mason called State Attorney Arthur Travis. "We have a whale in our sights," said Mason."

"Tell me more," said Travis.

Mason filled him in. "We are building the case. As I get more solid evidence, I will fill you in."

"Mason, I trust your judgment. This case is political dynamite."

"If we can prove it is criminal. You may discreetly check Burn's finances on your own. I expect new developments from High Hat."

Arthur laughed nervously. "I would not want to be Chiclets."

"My guess is that he is already dead and the gun he used broken into pieces and resting in the Schuykill or Delaware River."

"Isn't he related to High Hat?"

"Blood is not always thicker than water. The first rule of nature is self-preservation."

"True."

Mason hung up, hoping that justice would be served on all parties, but fearful that self-preservation would take more than one shape.

Mason lay in his recliner, trying to stay awake to see how the Phillies would manage to lose to the Red Sox. The Phils were up 3-2 in the ninth inning. They had blown a lot of late inning games. The Phillies rank number one all time in most games lost by a professional sport–over 11,000. Mason swore he watched half of them.

"Breaking News" banner flashed across the screen. PHILADELPHIA POLICE COMMISSIONER KNOX RESIGNS OVER CHARGES OF SEXUAL HARASSMENT.

The banner repeated three more times. In shock, Mason stared at the banner, his blood pressure rising.

Karen had gone to bed after dinner. He did not wake her. Knox was his hero, mentor and friend.

A reporter came on announcing that Deputy Chief of Police Cheryl Warden was acting Commissioner.

Mason liked Warden. The news prompted concerns for the Police,

Knox, the City and his case against corrupt ADAs. He called Travis.

"Did you hear about Knox?" asked Mason.

"Yes. This change puts a monkey wrench in our case. I need to sort it out."

"High Hat may be a problem. He disliked Knox and the feeling was mutual."

"What about Warden? Is she a straight shooter?" asked Travis.

"As far as I know she is clean. More information will surface tomorrow. Let's talk at the end of the day."

"Agreed."

Mason stared at the Phillies game. They had won. Two shocks in five minutes. He had a lot of thinking to do.

The next morning, Karen and Mason awoke simultaneously at six-thirty. He immediately told her about Knox's resignation.

"Oh, Dear God. What the hell is going on with our City? That man was a hero for handling the shooting of six policemen. Now he is out on a sexual harassment allegation? I need coffee," she said.

"Me too. I want to shower first," said Mason.

He stepped out of the shower, toweled himself, still weary from shock and a restless sleep when he heard Karen's scream.

He pulled on his shorts and rushed downstairs. She pointed to the kitchen window. The body of a black man dressed in white Nike's, blue jeans and a red a Phillies sweatshirt lay face up on his rear lawn.

Mason raced outside. A Glock lay at his side. He had a bullet hole in his right temple. The blood had caked dry on his head. Three white pieces of coated gum lay beside him.

"Chiclets," he said.

Karen started towards him, her arms wrapped across her chest. "Who is he? What happened?"

Mason put out his arms to stop her. "Stay away Karen. Our yard is now a crime scene."

"Is no place sacred in this City?" she asked, backing away.

High Hat had covered his tracks and squared Chuck's shooting.

Mason called Lester.

"Yes, Boss."

"I just found Chiclet's body in my back yard. I will call it in. Get a squad together, pick up High Hat and bring him to my office. I will be there after I clear the scene. Tell him he is a material witness and not under arrest."

Mason called Indira's cell phone and filled her in. "I want you to personally handle this one."

"Of course, Captain," she said.

"Run the ballistics of the gun on this scene to the ballistics at Chuck's murder."

"Yes, yes. I will do so."

"Check the inventory from Chuck's shooting. How many coffee cups were logged in?"

Mason's neighbors lined the property, muttering.

He scanned the crowd, realizing that he was the only black man present and he did not know any of them. Brotherly neglect.

Lester escorted High Hat into Mason's office. "Here he is Captain."

"Leave us," said Mason.

Lester dangled handcuffs. "Shall I cuff him?"

"No. Just leave until I call for you."

Mason motioned to a chair in front of his desk. "Sit down Holmes. We have a lot of catching up to do."

High Hat squeezed into the small arm-chaired seat. "You be looking well. I guess my old lady friend Karen is taking care of you like she took care of me before the accident."

"Leave her out of this. Let's talk about Chuck. Why did you order Chiclets to shoot him?"

High Hat waved his forefinger back and forth like a pendulum. "There you go jumping to conclusions. I had no fight with your boy Chuck."

"Who did?"

"Somebody else hired Chiclets to waste your boy.

"Payment was five grand. I am surprised that a smart man like you ain't figured out who did it."

"Maybe I have. So, why did you ice your half-brother and leave him on my property?"

"I did not shoot anyone. When was Chiclets sent to hell? Don't answer. Whenever it happened, I have an alibi."

Mason smiled. "You have always covered your butt. Why do you speculate he was left on my lawn?"

High Hat craned his neck, staring at the overhead lights. "Mayhap, someone is telling you to back off now that the score is even. An eye for an eye. Street Law, verse one, chapter one."

"How about Governing Law. Murder is illegal. How about God's law. Thou shalt not kill."

High Hat shook his head from side to side, grinning, his face aglow. "Mason, do you remember that TV show Law and Order? What we have in this City is Law and Disorder. Where there is no Justice, a man makes his own. Chiclets went out on his own when he shot Faraday. Nobody gave him the go-ahead. He broke the code of his street boss. In the court of the Street, there are no Rights that you cannot defend with a gun. When the hell are the damn fool politicians going to learn that they ain't the boss. They sold that position to their backers. Uncle Barry, Cousin Kevin, the whole bunch think they are the smartest people in the room. They got the Street sense of a manhole cover. You manage your District by the Book. I got my own Book. Look at what happened to your Chief, Knox. He was a good dude. He followed the so-called Good Book–the Law. He got bounced because he wanted some hoochy coo. Hah! Bill Clinton was a horn ball President. He got away with it."

High Hat extended his bad leg out. "I got in an accident that changed my life. I could have been an NBA forward, another Chocolate Thunder like Dawkins. But a cop chasing somebody ran into me. That Cop was you! That's how you met Karen. She ends up leaving me for the man that crippled me. Is that Justice?

Mason's iPhone buzzed. "Weapons match."

"That text confirms that the gun that killed Chuck is the same gun that killed Chiclets."

"What does that mean to me?" asked High Hat.

"Nothing. You can go."

High Hat struggled to his feet. "What do you see? Who shot my man Chiclets?"

"Chiclets did not kill himself and drag his own dead body to my lawn. Your boys shot him. He was bad for business. I hope you find peace before some ambitious stud puts two in *your* head."

"None of my dudes did the deed. Let me know who kilt the man and I will do my civic duty, according to the Law of Disorder. See you on the Street," signed, High Hat.

Mason called Indira. "I know the reason why Lester was not shot."

"What reason?"

"He was not in the car. He stood outside while Chiclets shot Chuck. Last night he shot Chiclets to cover it up. How many coffee cups were found in the car?"

"One. It had Chuck's prints on it."

"Check Lester's clothes for GSR. He may still have it on him from shooting Chiclets. Get two uniforms to drag him in for testing."

Lester sat at the table in the interview room. His eyes flitted around the room, like a fly eluding a swatter. Indira and Martha bookended him. Mason sat across from him, glaring like a cobra ready to strike.

"Why am I here?" asked Lester.

"You are here to tell us why you set up Chuck Faraday to be shot by Chiclets. You are here to admit to shooting Chiclets and leaving his body on my front lawn to try to fool me into believing High Hat Holmes shot him. You are to explain why there was only one coffee cup found in Chuck's car. You are to explain the GSR on your clothes. You are here to tell me how and why you became a murderer."

Lester hung his head in his hands for a long moment. He lifted his eyes to the ceiling. "Oh my good God. I want a Lawyer."

"When I tell High Hat that you shot his half-brother, you will need police protection, not a lawyer."

"I am leaving," said Lester.

Martha yanked him down by his shirt sleeve. "You have the right to remain silent. You have the right to an attorney. Anything you say may and will be used against you in a court of law."

She slapped handcuffs on him.

"What is your Lawyer's name and number?" she asked.

"Richard Burns. His brother is ADA Kevin Burns. His card is in my wallet."

Martha snatched the wallet and found the card. Mason pointed to the phone. "Call him."

"Wait. I can give you something big. I can give you Kevin Burns. He paid me to set up Chuck and make it look like a drive by, cop hating shoot. Chuck had the goods on Burns' scheme to ease up on felons for a price. Chuck made the mistake of telling Kevin to confess. He set himself up for the hit."

Mason lifted Lester by his shirt collar out of his chair. "You are worse than High Hat. You were just read the rights you were sworn to protect. How many pieces of silver were in it for you?"

"One hundred thousand, large."

"Take him away. I will call the new Commissioner and welcome her to her new job. God help her."

Karen snuggled against Mason on the sofa. The music channel played smooth jazz. Ella Fitzgerald sang Cole Porter's "Anything Goes."

"So here we are, two black people listening to a black woman sing a song written by a gay man who pretended to be straight. I would say we live in a diverse environment," she said.

Mason sipped his Merlot. "Add in French wine and you are on to something. I talked to Bridget. She knows Chuck died a hero. That is small consolation."

"Will Lester and Burns go to trial?"

"Your guess is as good as mine. It all depends on the politics, not the law. In that respect, High Hat Holmes has a point. Whose justice system is fairer? His or the City's?"

"Maybe, they are the same."

"Maybe."

"More wine?"

"Lots more, my Dear Lady. In vino veritas. In wine there is truth. I hope the adage *is* true. This City and me personally need a cask of wine for even a dram of truth and justice."

The Attar of Roses

Based on a true story

Rosalie Fabbiano brushed her long, jet black hair, added a touch of lipstick and eye shadow to her pretty, round face. She wanted to look pleasant for the trip to the Padre Pio Chapel in Barto, a rural hamlet near Allentown, Pennsylvania. She chose a modest, navy blue dress, drew her mother's miraculous medal around her neck and slipped on flat shoes. Her Grandfather Cosmo Fagbbiano had known the Archbishop of Allentown's father. The Archbishop of Allentown had pulled a few strings to allow her a one-time special favor as a last resort to save her father Enrico's life from Philadelphia chromosome-positive myeloid leukemia. Dad had been under treatment with Tasigna for two years. At first, the cancer had gone into remission, only to return in a virulent attack on his blood and bone marrow. According to the Doctors at the Cancer Center, he would die in three days barring a miracle. Rosalie was going for the miracle though she had stopped being a practicing Catholic in her senior year in high school. The stories of pedophilia in the Church had shred her allegiance to the Church. Her love for Enrico and her grieving mother, Theresa and younger sister Joanna overrode her contempt for hypocrisy, bad priests, and doctrine that disallowed birth control.

Rosalie had heard about the miracles in Padre Pio's name. The original miracle was the recovery of a young Italian girl named Vera. Time to test the legend. Time to show Mama the truth behind spiritual fiction.

Her mother and Joanna waited for her at the front door to their modest, split level home in Northeast Philly along Krewstown Road, just inside the Montgomery County border. Theresa's eyes were lined with tears and reddish circles. Her wan face crumpled in grief. Joanna stood tight-lipped, her thirteen-year-old face plastered with pain and disbelief, the sorrow of a child forced to face the horror of death of a loved one for the first time.

"God be with you Rosalie," said Theresa.

Joanna rushed to her sister's side and buried her face in her older sister's dress. "I will say another rosary for Daddy and you," said Joanna.

Rosalie took a handkerchief from her purse and swept away tears from Joanna's cheeks.

"Fabbiano, don't cry," said Rosalie.

The drive along Route 100 North passed through farmland, probably much like the farms of Foggia in Southeast Italy, the home province of Padre Pio. She mused to the sounds of Bruno Mars on her CD. She was on a fool's mission, but she owed it to Mama to try for a miracle.

Her in-car phone rang. The caller ID read, "Jason."

"Hello Jason."

"Hi, girlfriend. Where are you?"

"On a mission to God for Mama. Dad is near the end. Mama thinks if I rub his body with the glove of Padre Pio, Dad will beat the cancer. Nobody beats cancer, especially leukemia."

"Sorry about your Old Man. Sorry you have to go through the motions. Can we hook up tonight? I got some great IPA beer on ice. We can order in pizza and get cozy."

"Jack, you have the sensitivity of a honeymoon hard on. My father may die tonight. My mother needs me. Splash cold water on your dick and cool your hormones. I will call you after Dad passes."

"Okay. I got it. Call me when you are ready. My Atheist ass will not be saying you are in my thoughts and prayers."

"Good. Keep the faith, or lack of it."

The miracles of Padre Pio stemmed from the healing of the fifth child of Vera and Harry Colandra, born in Norristown just outside the north-west border of Philly in 1966. The child named Vera Marie was born with congenital defects that proffered a short and painful life. Her parents took the ailing child to visit Padre Pio in San Giovanni Rotondo, Italy. Padre Pio met with the child. Vera commented that Padre Pio emitted the sweet smell of roses. The Colandra family returned to the Philly area and Vera Marie made a full recovery. The healing inspired the Colandra family to erect the

Chapel in Barto and spread the Word of Padre Pio's miraculous healing.

The Padre Pio Museum and Chapel loomed over the flat land. The arched entry way showed her the route to her meeting with Emily Prozinski, curator. Mrs. Prozinski was a stout, square jawed lady with white hair and the visage of a happy woman. Her farmer's daughter hands shook Rosalie's hands, squeezing them into a crunchy ball of soft flesh. Emily's eyes sparkled behind wire-rimmed glasses.

"It is so good to meet you," she said in the foyer of the chapel. "Follow me."

Rosalie did not want a tour, but Emily appeared to be someone whom one argued with at your own peril.

They passed into an area where hundreds of votive candles shone in colorful array, each a symbol of a personal plea to God for help.

The portrait of Padre Pio hung from an elevated position, his white-grey beard surrounding a pleasant smile. He looked serene like a man on a blissful high, a heightened sense of reality. Tranquility in countenance and in his soul.

"Where is the halo?" she thought.

Over the main altar hung three carved marble reliefs.

"Who does the art work represent?" asked Rosalie, admiring the beauty of the paintings.

"To the left, we see Saint John the Baptist. The village of San Giovanni Rotondo celebrates his feast day every year on June 24th. He wears animal fur symbolizing his abandonment of his self to God's Will. His red raiment symbolizes his martyrdom. In the center, we see Father Pio's favorite, Our Lady of Grace holding the Christ Child. Father Pio often expressed supplication to the Holy Mother. To the right is Saint Paul holding a text, representing the author of sacred scripture. It is said that Saint Paul was Padre Pio's favorite writer of scripture. Over there is the portrait of Saint Francis of Assisi. His father was a Jewish merchant. Note the stigmata. And the young woman next to Saint Francis is Saint Massimana. She is no longer on the Church calendar of Saints, but the people of San Giovanni Rotondo still honor her. In the center of the altar stands our golden tabernacle topped with a gold crucifix."

"Saint Francis may not have approved of so much gold and wealth. He gave away his fortune, did he not?"

Emily raised her eyebrows in surprise and disapproval. "Indeed, he did. We use the beauty of the art and gold to enrich our religious environment, not our pocketbooks. Follow me."

Emily took her to a room at the rear of the Chapel. She unlocked a desk drawer and pulled out a worn, leathery glove. Here is Padre Pio's glove. Please guard it at all costs. My understanding is that you will have it returned by ten AM tomorrow. Your father must be a special man for the Archbishop to grant the use of the sacred glove."

"Dad is a wonderful man. My mother believes the glove may work a miracle for him."

"God works miracles through Padre Pio. The glove is a material reminder of Padre's closeness with God. The good Padre spoke to Jesus himself."

In a séance?

"I am sure they had a wonderful conversation. My mother requested I light a candle and make a small offering."

"Please do."

Rosalie folded the glove inside her purse. She picked out a yellow candle, Mom's favorite color. She lit it and watched it flame, remembering Jesus' words. "I am the way and the truth and the life ... he that believeth in me shall live forever."

Emily stood behind her, grim-faced, arms folded across her chest like a Sergeant at arms, glaring at the enemy.

"Thank you for your assistance, Mrs. Prozinski. I will take very great care with the Padre's glove."

"See that you do so."

Rosalie left the chapel feeling as though the smiling eyes of Padre Pio and the wrath of Emily were riveted on her in equal measure. She had learned that a religious zealot was as dangerous as she was devout.

She called Theresa. "Mom. I have the glove. Meet me at the hospital in an hour. Bring Joanna."

She headed to the hospital feeling that this would be her last day with Enrico.

Doctor Arjun Patel was on duty. A tall, well-built Indian man, with piercing black eyes and a constant frown of seriousness, greeted her.

"I am afraid he may not make it through the night. His urine is brown, a sign that the contaminated blood has fully metastasized," said Patel. "Your mother and sister await."

Patel escorted her into Enrico's room. Her father lay quietly, an intravenous tube filling his arm with morphine. His once swarthy pallor had melted into a sallow shade of gray. His bushy eyebrows needed trimming. The mother, Theresa, sat at the bedside. Joanna slumped in a chair in the far corner.

"We have made him as comfortable as possible. I shall stay the night."

"Thank you, Doctor," said Theresa.

They closed the door. Rosalie handed the glove to her mother. "Here Mama. Rub Dad with it."

"We shall take turns. Rosalie you rub his arms. Joanna, you rub his chest. I will rub his legs. Pray that Padre Pio looks upon him and cures him."

Fat chance thought Rosalie.

Enrico lay quietly through the gentle massage. Rosalie kneaded her father's arms, once so strong and muscular. "He used to hug me to death," she said. "I will squeeze you like Charmin, he told me a thousand times."

Joanna took her turn, barely touching his hairy chest before lapsing into tears. "God bless you, Daddy," she said.

Theresa sobbed as she finished rubbing his thin, emaciated legs. "My strong man. May Padre Pio save you."

They sat in a vigil until ten PM. Patel visited the room every hour. "I see no progress. Please go home all of you. I shall be here on duty. He will not be alone. I will call you if there is any change in his condition."

The family left, grieving, resigned to Enrico's death. Padre Pio had not intervened.

Rosalie awoke to the rising sun. Joanna and Theresa were asleep in their bedrooms. She needed coffee, a shower, and a toasted bagel with cream cheese. At seven, all three were seated around the kitchen table when the house phone rang.

"Answer it Rosalie," said Theresa. "I cannot."

"Hello."

"Come immediately," said Dr.Patel.

"Is my father dead?"

"Just come now."

The three women entered Enrico's room, unsure what they would find.

Enrico was sitting up in his bed, smiling. His pallor had ripened into a russet hue.

They rushed to his side.

"Daddy!" said Joanna in tears.

Theresa blessed herself. "Mother of God. Thank you!" She hugged him.

Rosalie stood with her back to the wall, feeling faint. "What is going on Doctor?" she asked, afraid of the answer.

"Last night, on a hunch I tripled his dose of Tasigna. He reacted immediately. Strangely, at the moment he perked up, I saw a heavy-set man in tan robes standing beside him. And I caught a whiff of roses. I know the smell because my mother used rose water."

"I am starving," said Enrico. "Can I get some breakfast?"

"All you want," said Dr. Patel.

The next morning, Rosalie trekked to Barto to return the glove. During the ride under a gleaming sun, her mind floated from her first rencounter at the Chapel to her moments running the glove over her father's body. She felt stunned, disbelieving as she entered the Chapel. She knelt at the altar of candles, lit one and said the Hail Mary.

The strong hand of Mrs. Prozinski landed on her shoulder.

"Was your trip successful?"

Rosalie nodded. "Yesterday, we rubbed my father's body with the glove of Padre Pio. He awoke this morning alive, vibrant as a young man. I cannot believe what I have seen with my own eyes. And the doctor swore he smelled the attar of roses. Did I witness a miracle?"

"Yes. Father Pio is real. You have been blessed to see God's handiwork."

"I feel like a newborn learning she is alive. There is a god, isn't there?"

Mrs. Prozinski put out her hand. “Give me the glove please. God’s work is never done.”

Rosalie handed her the soft leather glove feeling she had shaken hands with Padre Pio.

Leaving, she paused in front of Padre Pio’s portrait. The smiling friar seemed alive. He would always be with her. She would always remember the attar of roses.

Bad Genes

Jeffrey Maloney was torn while considering his Master's thesis subject at Temple Journalism School between the Decline of the Philly Mob and the Frankford Slasher, a serial killer never caught by Philly Police. Both subjects had merit as Journalistic subject matter and plenty of documented historical facts to draw upon. Who better to consult than his retired Great Uncle Mike Maloney, his Grandfather's older brother? At the time of the murder and rape of nine women, Uncle Mike was stationed at the twenty-sixth Police District on East Girard Avenue. He worked the Slasher case as part of a team. The District was under enormous pressure from the neighbors, the DA, the Mayor, and the newspapers. The perp had killed more women than Jack the Ripper.

Jeffrey, in his research, found that in 1990, the Police arrested a black man named Leonard Christopher for the murder of forty-six-year-old Carol Dowd. The police named Christopher the Frankford Slasher, thereby closing nine cases. The only problem was that a tenth victim was slashed while Christopher was in jail awaiting trial. Christopher was convicted of Dowd's murder and sentenced to life without parole. The real Frankford Slasher was never found.

Uncle Mike was a Grand Marshall for the Ancient Order of Hibernians. Their Lodge on East Girard was a popular watering hole for retired Irish policemen. No Italians, Jews, Poles, Blacks, Hispanic, Protestants, Muslims, Gays, Atheists or Quakers were listed in the membership logs.

He trod up the hardwood steps to the Club's private office. The Irish and American flags hung behind a mahogany desk where Uncle Mike was waiting for him. A bottle of Jameson Black Label and two liquor glasses greeted Jeffrey as he entered, laptop in hand. Uncle Mike was a powerfully built man, a wrestler in high school, a street fighter of renown and one smart cop.

He believed in the Law, Jesus Christ, the Catholic Church and his beloved family of four police brothers, one nun and one high school Special Ed teacher, their sons and daughters and the family at large.

"Hello Jeffrey."

Jeffrey shook hands with the much older man whom clasped his hand in a vice.

"Hello Uncle Mike. Thanks for seeing me."

Uncle Mike poured Jeffrey one finger high of liquor. He poured himself two fingers. "Slainte!"

They clicked glasses. "Slainte!" said Jeffrey, sipping his shot while Uncle Mike downed his in one quick gulp.

Jeffrey sat on a round-back wooden chair feeling like a young boy in the presence of a living legend. The man had more decorations on the walls of the office than a Christmas tree.

"What brings you here?"

"Uncle Mike, I am about to write my thesis on either the history of the Mob in Philly or the case of the Frankford Slasher. I cannot decide which to choose for a topic. I know you worked the Slasher case. My research suggests that Leonard Christopher was not the Slasher. He is the wrong color and a tenth slashing occurred while Christopher was in jail. No charges were brought against him for being the slasher. He was convicted of murdering the Dowd woman and sentenced to life without parole. What light can you shed on the case?"

Mike gave him a thumbs up. "You have presented a well-thought out question. My guess is that you would prefer to write about the Slasher. You grew up in Frankford. He terrorized the whole bloody neighborhood. People hung signs on telephone poles saying–find the slasher before he finds your loved ones–the Mob is old history since Angelo Bruno was murdered. I can still see the newspaper picture of Bruno shot dead inside his car, his bloody mouth open as a blow fish taking bait."

Jeffrey finished his shot, a little embarrassed that he had not chugged it. "Part of what intrigues me, is that in the last forty years, Philly has witnessed so many serial killings. Marie Noe killed eight of her children. You had Gary Heidnik, the Kallingers, Joseph and his son Michael. Hell, Heidnik murdered his namesake fourteen-year-old son."

"Then there was the case of Harrison Graham. The bodies of seven women were found in the basement of Harrison Graham in the late eighties. Ted Bundy attended Temple. It makes my skin crawl thinking I am walking the same stairs and corridors that sick bastard walked. Let's not forget the Kensington Strangler named Antonio Rodriguez. The worst of all was Kermit Gosnell who murdered newborn children. Hollywood made a movie about Gosnell. These killers had nothing in common except the fact that they were Philadelphians. They murdered at Will. Why? Why in Philly? Is there something in the water that breeds murder like an airborne disease?"

Uncle Mike poured a second shot. "Another?"

"No thanks. My tolerance for whiskey is well below family standards."

Uncle Mike tossed back a second shot. "Ah, the nectar of the gods."

"Who do you think was the Slasher?"

"No one can say for sure. The heat was so heavy on us that we focused on the bird at hand in Rodriguez. He killed Carol Dowd for sure. His arrest conveniently put to rest the hysteria over the Slasher."

"Did you have any other suspects?"

Uncle Mike's blue eyes twitched. "None. We had none."

Jeffrey's stomach tightened. His uncle was lying. Jeffrey poured himself and his uncle a shot. "Is there a reason you want me to stop pursuing the Strangler case?"

"Laddy, I said no such thing. My fear is that opening a closed case will only arouse the Police Haters in the City to anarchy. Six policemen were shot this year in Nicetown. The citizenry of Nicetown threw bottles and rocks at the very officers protecting them from an active shooter. We do not need to set off a stick of dynamite, do we Lad?"

"A Journalist's job is to find and report the Truth. Honestly and impartially."

"Do your report on the mob. The bloody Italians like publicity. More than their homemade wine. Give them a snoot full. Maybe you will turn the thesis into a book and make a mint. You can title it the Philly Sopranos."

Jeffrey laughed. "You have quite an imagination, Uncle Mike. It certainly is tempting to go for the money."

"Do you want something more than fame and a million dollars? You are an Idealist, a loony tune writer. There is money and power and nothing else worth pursuing in this world."

"I want the truth. I checked the newspaper files on the tenth killing. The prostitute was Shirley Gibson. You interviewed her. You know the truth. Give me the real story."

Uncle Mike stared at Jeffrey, a mean scowl.

"You should have been a detective. I interviewed Shirley's pimp. His name was Jeremy Wilson. I liked the bastard for killing her. But I had no proof."

"Why did you like him?"

"All of the girls killed by the Slasher worked for Jeremy's competitors. It looked like a turf war."

Jeffrey's eyes rolled around the room. He swooned thinking of the implications. "What cops were in on the prostitution ring?"

Uncle Mike slammed his fist on the table so hard the whiskey bottle fell on its side spilling the precious liquor. "Damn. Look at what you made me do." He righted the bottle as if he were a priest raising a chalice at Mass.

Jeffrey leaned across the desk and whispered,

"Kill the girls and you shut down the money stream. It was a street war. The papers reported the death of Jeremy Wilson as a robbery murder.

"What went down?"

"The case is closed."

"Wilson killed those girls, didn't he? And the street exacted justice."

"I have no idea how you could concoct such a tale and call it journalism. It's fake news."

"I cannot corroborate my theory of the case. It will remain unsolved. Just tell me if I am right or wrong. Tell me, damnit."

Uncle Mike drank a long draft directly from the bottle. "The case is closed."

"The Slasher case is closed. But I can write my thesis on political influence versus Justice. The real crime here is the murder of justice for political expediency. "

"That is quite a fable. Perhaps ye should change your name to Aesop."

Jeffrey laughed. "That is a good idea for a working title. Aesop and the prostitutes of Kensington."

"Why did you come here?"

"I came to test my theory. I came to see if I could trust you. Mission accomplished. I'll go now before I make you spill any more liquid courage."

"Boy, I put my life on the line for forty years. In my line of work, a man makes choices. Decisions are not easy. There are always unforeseen consequences."

"Spare me the lecture. I get enough at Temple." He headed toward the door.

"What would you have done?"

Jeffrey spun around. "Who killed Jeremy Wilson?"

Uncle Mike paused for a long moment. He cast a red-faced glare that Jeffrey knew was a sign of fury, eighty-six proof and straight from the gut.

"Your father shot the slimy prick. We knew Rodriguez was not the Slasher. He copped to killing Carol Dowd. We had no need to charge him beyond what he did. We staged it to look like we had a viable suspect to draw out the real culprit. It was your father's idea and it worked. We used a policewoman to impersonate a prostitute. When Wilson attacked her, a policeman in plain clothes killed him. The street war was over. The Slasher killings stopped. The City breathed easy for at least one night."

Jeffrey recoiled as if shot. "No way. You are lying."

"Son, the real world is a messy place. Your father saved lives and put the City's anxieties to bed. He is a bloody hero. And I will go to my grave denying I ever told you the truth."

"Damn it to hell. Dad shot that squirrel?"

"He did, and I covered for him. You have a choice. Reopen a closed case and incriminate your family or go in a different direction. You decide."

"I will."

"Do the right thing, Jeffrey."

Jeffrey walked out the door and down the stairs to the barroom of the AOH. Two men were hoisting whiskey glasses. "Up the Republic" shouted a stout, older man wearing a stick pin of the Irish and American flags pinned to the lapel of his green blazer. The other man was much younger, a dead ringer for the older man. They wore ceremonial kilts, plaid vests, and black tams. Father and son. A continuum of inherited-values.

The title of his thesis flashed across his mind. "Bad Genes. The hereditary disease of political influence and its effect on Social Justice."

Somebody had to stop the madness of serial injustice to save this City. Somebody.

He opened the door of the AOH, walked outside and took a deep breath. The air was as fresh as a coal mine. The roar of traffic, horns blaring, impatience was deafening. To find the truth amid chaos and lost history and political forces arrayed in a circling of the wagons smacked of tilting at windmills.

He had buried his father once. Should he resurrect him to bury him again with dishonor?

Jeffrey shuffled along the trash strewn streets, wondering if anybody but he really cared about a dead felon unjustly slain.

"What should I do, Dad?" he whispered in the noisy afternoon air.

No answer came.

He trudged ahead past a homeless man crouched under a tattered blanket, his scruffy beard hiding most of his pock-marked face. A woolen cap pulled over his ears. His dirty, gnarled hand outstretched. He smelled of urine and cheap whiskey. Jeff handed the man a dollar.

"Eat something," he said.

"Go screw yourself," said the man.

Jeffrey laughed. "If I write the truth, you and I may be friends someday."

The man shoved the dollar in his corduroy pants. "Then don't write nothing. Only fools tell the truth to a world of liars."

"Well said, Mister. Well said."

Jeffrey started away as the homeless man called out. "What are you going to do?"

"Write the truth. Save me a spot next to you."

"You are a damned fool."

"Yes, I am."

Cinder Ella Met A Fella

Based on a real-life Incident

Mabel Mae Williams was mad as hell. Cynthia Ella Olinsky was mad as hell. To save money, the State of Pennsylvania had eliminated cafeteria aides during lunch hours at all public schools.

"Don't those damn fools realize they are putting our kids in danger?" asked Mabel.

"The almighty State of Pennsylvania took over the City's schools to make them better. How the hell does turning lunchrooms into war zones make them better?" said Cindy.

They were sitting at Mabel's kitchen table over iced tea and Tastykake fruit pies. Mabel's long black hair, matched her dark skin, deep set eyes screwed narrow in a lethal grimace. Cindy's blond, Irish-Catholic curls circled her cherubic blue eyes and crimson sneer. She stood five-two and feared no one, not even her six-foot two iron worker ex-husband, Joe Klotz.

"We have worked for over a decade in the cafeteria at FDR High School and we know what goes on and can only imagine the chaos of unsupervised lunchrooms. Kids will see the lack of authority as a license to fool around, fight, smoke, whatever. If the adults are not serious, why should they behave?" said Cindy.

"We got to fight this," said Mabel.

"How? We are two divorced women with no political ties and no money," said Cindy.

"We need allies. Parents, teachers, administrators. We need to get the word out to fight the State. What is the axiom? It takes a village."

"Wait a minute. Maybe we can enlist somebody who knows how to raise support for a cause."

"Who?"

"How about that dude on television who is always helping the little guy against City Hall?"

"Yes. Frank Furion. He gives an aspirin a headache when he jumps on the politicians."

"Let's call him now. I bet his phone number is on his website."

Furion answered immediately." Hello. Frank Furion here."

"Mr. Furion. My name is Mabel Mae Williams and I have you on speaker with my co-worker, Cindy Olinsky. We are calling to ask for your help to get the Governor to rehire the safety patrol people he let go. He made our school kids unsafe. We are longtime employees of the School District and we want to get the Governor to change his mind before somebody gets hurt."

"Oh. What did you have in mind? A protest? A sit in?"

"This is Cindy Olinsky, Mister Furion. I just had an idea. Since this protest involves lunchrooms, I think a hunger strike may be a better form of protest. Hell, I *need* to lose weight."

"If you ladies are serious, be in my office on Broad Street in one hour. I know about the Governor's mean-spirited cuts. I personally do not like the cruel S O B. But if you are triflers, do not show up."

"We are serious as a junkyard dog on rabies," said Cindy.

Furion laughed at the allusion to the old Jim Croce song lyrics.

"Yeah. And I am badder than old King Kong. See you in an hour," he said and hung up.

The women high-fived. "Hot damn, grand slam," said Mabel.

"I will drive," said Cindy.

"We'll split the parking and gas," said Mabel Mae.

"Deal."

Frank Furion, 41, was Philly born, bred, educated and lived in South Philly all his life. He'd worked his way through night school at LaSalle, majoring in communications. On weekends, he sang in clubs, weddings, any place he could make a buck. He made a lot of contacts, winning people over with his charm, good looks and Sinatra like tenor style. His voice and tenacious, "in your face" South Philly nature landed him a job on a local radio station followed by a feature show on local television. His nickname-

Franky Fury was well earned. He played the angry young man role to the hilt of his microphone. Frank also despised the hypocrisy and greed infesting the body politic. The call from the two women lit up his imagination. He could palpably smell the power of the story. City kids put at risk by misers in Harrisburg was not a new tale. Having the two mothers sitting in his office ready to go on a hunger strike was a gem of a story sent by Providence.

Mabel wagged her finger at the nameless Politicians. "I am a mother. I am a mother to those kids. I feed them. I listen to their daily trials and tribulations. They deserve protection."

Cindy was as pretty as a rose in bloom. Frank had a lifelong attraction to Irish girls with pale skin and blue sapphire eyes.

"Mabel is right, Mister Furion."

"You ladies may call me Frank."

"Okay. Please use our first names. Cindy and Mabel Mae," said Cindy.

Frank leaned forward; his white shirt sleeves rolled up. "Do you ladies remember the story of Mahatma Gandhi, the Indian man who brought the British Empire to its knees. His fight started with a hunger strike. He won India its independence. Maybe if we think like Ghandi, we can win your battle."

"What should we do to get started?" asked Mabel.

"Whoa. Slow down. I need to ask some tough questions. You two will be in the public eye. Is there anything criminal in your backgrounds?"

Mabel threw back her head, shook her long hair and laughed out loud. "My transgression was marrying a no-good bum. I kicked him to the curb when I found out he was running some skank ass whore from Nicetown. My boy is in the Marines in Afghanistan."

Cindy dropped her head for a moment. She looked directly into Frank's eyes with the sad countenance of a woman who had fought her way through life and had never won. "I am married to a drunk. He likes VO more than sex. Is being stupid a crime? If so, I am the whole South Philly mob in one package. I have a daughter away at school in Millersville studying to be a teacher. Ironic, huh?"

"No arrests, no drugs is good news. They cannot impugn your character. I researched the layoff. Over twelve hundred people lost their jobs. The economic impact on those families is part of the problem. We have a Republican Governor ruling over a Democratic city. This layoff is political payback."

Cindy and Mabel exchanged glances. "I did not think of that," said Mabel.

"They won't admit it, but do you think they would have laid off safety guards in a white school district so readily?"

"No," said Mabel.

"Hell no," said Cindy.

"The key here is to paint the decision the State made to be based on political reasons and not economic reasons. To get the Public on our side, we must show the social injustice behind the State's layoffs. You ladies will become the face of mothers struggling to protect their children. We must ignite outrage to force change. Are you up to this task?"

"Yes, I am," said Mabel.

"Ditto," said Cindy.

"Me too. Let's go get the bastards. First, I suggest you two camp out in front of the Governor's Philly office on Broad Street. Bring beach chairs so you are comfortable. Bring water but no food. It is hot for June and we do not want you dehydrated. The sit in should go from eight am to eight pm."

"Where do we go for poddy breaks?" asked Mabel.

"The Governor's office is one possibility. There is also a hotel across Broad Street. I will make sure they accommodate you. Free publicity carries a lot of weight."

"When do we start?" asked Mabel.

Frank checked the calendar on his iPhone. "How about eight am to eight pm beginning on the Seventeenth. You will get noticed by the rush hour traffic on Broad Street. Your station will be only two blocks from the Headquarters of the Philadelphia School Board. I will get cameras to cover the sit-in. I will also appeal to parents to join the hunger strike. The more people we attract, the better. We will plan on staying on the strike until Harrisburg wakes up or the public outcry is so loud, they hear the hue and cry in the Governor's Office a hundred miles away. I will get the Union to support us."

"Do you think this will work?" asked Cindy.

"I honestly do not know," said Frank.

Mabel stood up, feeling proud and determined. "We will do our part, Frank. You do your part and get us the notoriety we need to get the State to put the safety staff back to work."

They shook hands and departed. Outside, Mabel turned to Cindy, a worried furrow creased her forehead. "Cindy, please tell old Mabel we are doing the right thing."

"When you got nothing, you got nothing to lose."

Mabel chuckled. "I know that's true."

Frank Furion had calls to make. First, he called UNITE HERE, the labor Union that represented the laid off aides. They talked for half an hour trying to come up with a slogan, They chose "Fast for Safe Schools."

Placards to follow by opening day of the fast.

He called his cousin, Joe Dimon, whose son was a student at Woodrow Wilson School and convinced him to join the Fast. He also recruited a former co-worker, Grace McDowell. Grace could stop traffic with her long legs and strawberry blond hair. She had two kids in William Penn grade school in Northeast Philly.

He hoped the Fast would work soon. Mabel looked strong enough to hang in. Cindy looked pale, worn out from a bad marriage.

She needed protection as much as the students.

He took an Uber home and fell asleep on his couch after eating a leftover cheesesteak and two glasses of Chianti. Was Cindy as lonely as he?

On the morning of June 17, 2013, Cindy rose early. She showered for a full twenty minutes, grateful for soothing water to ease her worrisome mind. She had never been in the limelight, except for a rare occasion like her wedding and her daughter Myra's graduation from Central High School. She dressed in light gray pants, a yellow cotton blouse and sandals. She sprayed on Chanel perfume. The mirror reflected a pretty, wrinkle free middle-aged woman. She did not want to disappoint Frank.

Mabel and Cindy converged on Frank Furion and two others seated in beach chairs outside the office of the governor of Pennsylvania. Cindy and Mabel greeted Joe and Grace.

The sun baked the five of them, portending a long hot day. A television camera man filmed the group while Frank used a microphone to talk to his on-air audience.

"Welcome to the sit-in by employees and parents protesting the State's decision to release over twelve hundred noontime aides who keep peace and order in our public schools. Let me introduce the two ladies who had the courage to call for this sit down. They are Mabel Mae Williams and Cindy Olinsky. The parents supporting these brave ladies are Joseph Dimon and Grace McDowell."

He placed the hand-held mic toward Mabel Mae and Cindy. "Ladies, please tell the audience why you are taking on the State of Pennsylvania."

Mabel spoke first. "The State has put our children in danger. We are here to get the State to rescind their layoff and put the aides back on the job."

"What say you, Cindy?"

"As a mother and a long-time cafeteria worker, I know our kids need protection from elements that would use unsecured, unsupervised areas to sell drugs and enlist kids in gangs. Over my dead body."

"Wow! Strong words from two determined ladies. What say you, Ms. McDowell and Mr. Dimon?"

"We support these women and agree with their position," said Grace.

"Amen to that," said Joe.

The camera did a close-up of Joe. "I must add that the Unite Here Labor Union also supports this sit in. It may be a long hot summer for these ladies, but I am betting on them to get Harrisburg to put aside politics and protect the children of Philadelphia. You can join this fight to protect our school kids. Tweet me @ Fury on Fire. Tweet the Governor and your State legislators. You can also announce your support by posting on Facebook–Fast for Safe Schools.com. Join this battle, please. The kids you save may be your own. I am Frank Furion. Always with Philly."

Frank handed the camera man the microphone. "Come together every one. We need a group hug."

Frank put his arms around Cindy and Mabel, squeezing them close to him."

"This is just the beginning. If we stick together, we will win. I am going now. See you this afternoon," said Frank. He patted Cindy's shoulder and nodded a tacit approval.

The day dragged on. Passersby stopped and asked questions about the sit-in, mainly supporting the protest. Nearly all offered support, except one elderly lady who had a State ensign on her pants suit lapel. She cast a disapproving glare and railed, "Why should I pay to baby sit someone else's child?"

Mabel growled, like a petulant tigress. "Because it's the right thing to do. Deny children safety and you deny them a future."

The woman said, "God helps those who help themselves."

Mabel clambered out of her seat, her fists balled up. "Lady, you best shut up right here and now."

Cindy grabbed Mabel's arm. "No violence. We will lose if we hit one person."

Mabel pulled her arm free. "Sorry. I am hot and she pissed me off."

"Me too."

After lunch when passing cars started beeping their horns in support. Drivers gave their thumbs up. The recognition surprised Cindy and Mabel. Frank must be getting the word out. He was the first man she had met in a decade that impressed her with his honesty.

Frank appeared around five PM, smiling like he had just won a Pulitzer Prize.

"We are gaining support from the Press and media. The politicians will see the tide rolling in your favor. This battle may be over sooner than later."

The Fast kept on until the twenty fourth of June. The heat and the fast wore on Mabel. She could not get out of bed. Her neighbors called 911. Mabel refused to get into the ambulance. She called Cindy. "Sister C., I am all worn out. I need a break. I am so sorry."

Cindy replied, "I got your back. Frank is calling for volunteers to join us. We will carry on. You get well. I am not stopping until we win."

Frank grabbed Cindy's phone. "Mable Mae. This is Frank. We will not abandon Cindy Ella. You get some rest. My sources tell me the State is feeling a lot of heat. We must hang in. I will not quit either."

Cindy gently retrieved her iPhone. Frank looked a foot taller. "Thank you, Frank. Don't let me down."

Frank rested his hands on her shoulders. "How could I let down a heroine."

"Others have."

Two days later, Cindy awoke, her body sweating so badly her night shirt clung to her chest and back. She stumbled into the bathroom, turned on the shower at lukewarm. The shower revived her enough for her to down orange juice and a small bowl of oatmeal. Her stomach ached as she swallowed the meager breakfast. She drew on fresh shorts and an old Eagles tee shirt over her bra. She packed water bottles and ice in her refrigerated carry bag.

The drive down Broad Street seemed to take longer than usual. She parked across the street from the sit-in location. The air was stifling. The heat index blew past one hundred degrees around noon. She drank her water and splashed half a bottle on her face.

"Are you alright?" asked Grace.

"I am fine." She had to pee. She rose up, took one step and collapsed at Grace's feet.

The EMTs revived her. "You will be fine Ma'am," said a tall black man in uniform. We will take you to Jefferson Hospital for a check."

"No. I am staying here. Get me to my chair."

"Ma'am, you passed out. You need to get out of this heat."

"Is hell any hotter? If I leave my post, I should go to hell for desertion."

Frank arrived, after Grace's call. He knelt beside her. "Cindy. We need you alive. I will get volunteers to fill in for you. We will not abandon the sit in."

Cindy wept. "I failed you. I failed the kids. I failed Mabel."

Frank cupped her face in his hands. "No. You just need a break. Joe will drive you home. Rest for a couple of days. Come back swinging. We are winning."

Cindy clutched his hand. "Do not lie to me, Frank. Promise me you will not leave me alone as others have done."

"I swear I will keep the sit-in going until we win."

"I hope you are telling me the truth."

"Bet on it."

"I have already bet on you. Now get me home."

Three days later, fifteen politicians including a State Senator joined the protest. The newspapers praised Mabel's sacrifice and Cindy's resolve. A group of strikers walked into the Governor's office with a petition signed by over one thousand signatures demanding the State reinstate the aides at a cost of one hundred and forty million dollars. The war was over–almost.

By mid August, the State had not rehired the aides. Feeling betrayed, Cindy and Mabel and Frank called a meeting of all supporters. They met outside the State office, all wearing their tee shirts. Reporters, TV cameras, and radio staffs huddled around them.

Frank opened his microphone. "The State has failed to keep its promise to fund the rehires. These ladies and I ask you to intercede and call out the dishonest bastards. They need to hear your voice and feel the toe of your shoe up their butts. Will you help us?"

"The crowd roared a resounding, "Yes!"

Frank took to the air waves, blasting the Legislature. The Inquirer and Daily News issued front page calls for a federal intervention. The temperature in Harrisburg was hotter in the air-conditioned legislative chambers than on the concrete streets of Philly.

On August fourteenth, over one hundred people marched on the School District headquarters on Broad Street. They carried placards reading, "Let us keep our kids safe."

Frank ordered a hundred tee shirts emblazoned, "Fast for Safe Schools." The strikers wore them to highlight the Cause.

The bad Press lit a fire under the State. On August twenty-fourth, the State capitulated. The legislature authorized the funds to rehire one thousand one hundred and thirty-six aides.

The Philly ladies had won.

Cindy and Mabel celebrated with champagne at Mabel's home. Joe, Grace, and a dozen supporters attended. The crowd was as bubbly as the Great Western champagne. They gathered around Mabel and Cindy singing, "For they are jolly good fellows. For they are jolly good fellows, that no one can deny."

Cindy felt a renewed pride in herself. She had achieved a measure of satisfaction. She felt like Providence had guided her from the realm of blank obscurity to a home in the sunshine. Where was Frank?

Near the end of the evening, her I phone rang.

"Hello."

"Hey Cindy Ella. This is Prince charming. Sorry I could not stop by Mabel Mae's for the shindig. The cable news networks are all over me. Thanks to you."

"We missed you. Joe and Grace were there."

"My dear Lady C, the whole city is celebrating. Say, how about you and I have a victory dinner tomorrow night at The Victor Café. The name seems appropriate. I can pick you up at seven."

Cindy shook the phone. "Are you asking me out on a date?"

"Why not? We work well together. How about it Cinderella? They can sing an old South Philly ditty. Cinderella met a fella."

"You just made that up?"

"Look at it this way. You just pulled off a miracle. You deserve a glass slipper."

"It's a date."

She walked back to Mabel Mae, tears welling in her blue eyes.

"What's wrong Girlie?" asked Mabel Mae.

Cindy poured a glass of champagne. "God works in mysterious ways."

Mabel laughed out loud. "I will bet my life that was Frank on the phone asking you for a date."

"How did you know?"

Mabel held up her glass. "You two been playing goo-goo eyes for three weeks."

"I am too old for goo-goo eyes."

"Nope. You are as young as you feel. Today we took the cake. Tomor row, you get the icing."

Cindy raised her glass. "Attention everybody. This day the kids won and so did we. And the City of Philadelphia. Cheers to All."

Her mind buzzed a new ditty. "Cinderella met a fella."

The City of Brotherly Love

Non-identical twins, Malcom and Henry Penfield were born on April Thirtieth, nineteen-seventy-five, the last day of the Vietnam War. Malcolm preceded Henry by four minutes. Legend has it they came out of the womb screaming–at each other. Their parents, Joel and Bernice, had no other children due to complications arising from their birth.

The parents had married in their thirties and both were over thirty-five when the boys were born, making the cessation of pregnancy more palpable for them.

As fraternal twins, the brothers were designated to pursue separate paths, as do any siblings born separately. Malcolm was right side of the brain dominant, while Henry was left side dominant. Never were the twain to meet in civil discourse.

Early on, Malcolm colored with crayons while Henry built houses with tiny bricks in a pattern. From grade school through high school, they matched straight A report cards. Neither wanted to surrender intellectual superiority, the Grail of parental approval with bragging rights and parental smiles to the one with the better grades.

Brotherly love was replaced with brotherly envy by the time they were ten years old.

The gap widened at thirteen when twelve-year-old, blond, Marian Schmidt, a next-door neighbor, allowed Malcolm a quick kiss on her tightly pursed lips. Henry tried to kiss her, but she turned her face away.

"Oooooh. You are so gross, Henry."

Malcolm laughed, chiding Henry. "Only a blind girl would kiss your face."

Henry curled his fists, but did not strike his brother, lest he enrage his parents who clearly favored Malcolm.

Matters worsened in high school when Henry earned a starting running back position on the Germantown Academy football team while Malcolm was on the cusp of getting cut from the team.

Standing on the practice field, Henry took great satisfaction when the coach announced Malcolm was the final cut. Malcolm stomped his cleats and cursed the sky.

"It's not fair. I deserve a spot on this team."

"You can always try out for the girls field hockey team, Malcolm. They wear skirts," said Henry. Guffaws erupted from the team.

Red-faced Malcolm charged his brother, driving his shoulder into Henry, sending them both to the ground. Henry rolled Malcolm over, landing on top of Malcolm. Henry rammed his fist into Malcolm's nose. Blood spurted over Malcolm's face and chest.

"Fight nice boys. You are brothers," said the coach breaking up the tussle.

Henry leaped up, his fists balled in anger.

"Your nose sprung a leak, Brother M.," sneered Henry.

"Malcolm scowled like a wounded animal. "Go to hell."

"Shake hands," said the coach.

"No," said the brothers in unison.

Malcolm earned a National Merit Scholarship to the University of Pennsylvania. His goal was to receive a Doctorate in American Literature and to become a Professor at Penn. He beamed with pride, strutting about the House, avoiding Henry except for the occasional reminder that he scored 1492 in the college Boards. "Columbus and I are 1492 men," was his favorite dig.

Henry attended Drexel University on a five-year Co-Op program majoring in Construction Management. He attended classes for six months and worked at Farrell construction, a paving contractor for six months. By the time Henry graduated with a B average, Straight As Malcolm was halfway to completing his Master of Arts degree.

Their quarrels elevated as Malcolm espoused left wing Democratic positions while Henry argued for capitalism and Conservative values.

Thanksgiving dinner in nineteen-ninety-nine set the stage for a full confrontation between pro Clinton Malcolm and Republican Henry. Malcolm lived at the family residence in Chestnut Hill while Henry had moved into a rented Carriage house.

Both young men were fully grown, handsome and dating girls. Neither man dare bring their lady friends to the dinner, fearful the other brother would inflict barbs, snickers, and sarcastic remarks on the girls.

Thanksgiving swept in on the wings of Autumn winds, splashing a chill across the half acre property. The two story, stone Dutch-Colonial home was complete with dormers offering large windows and white frame shutters. White columns graced the front entrance, affording the home a Hallmark card look.

Henry arrived at one o clock, just in time for the first football game. He shuffled off his black leather jacket, revealing his tight vee neck plaid vest. His fitted jeans clung to his muscular legs. He could still play football.

He handed his mother a bouquet of red roses, her favorite flowers and pecked her cheek. A return hug from her was not in the offering. She held up her cheek for a perfunctory kiss. "The flowers are beautiful. You should save your money."

"You are welcome, Mother," he said in a low whisper at her retreating back, an apron wrapped around her thin body. Her workouts were more home-based since Joel's illness. She dared not leave him alone lest he wander off as he had before.

Henry walked into the den overlooking the rear yard. Dad sat in a leather recliner. His white shirt covered by a red cardigan University of Pennsylvania sweater, baggy over his rounded shoulders. Oak paneled walls and hardwood flooring gleamed in the sunshine pouring through the glass doors to the patio. The brick fireplace cast a warm glow across the den, its seams creased the bricks with milk white mortar. Henry had suggested black mortar. Malcolm suggested white to match Penn colors. White won.

The dark mortar would have been a more appropriate match and would have accented the bricks, thought Henry. A Penn pennant and a Drexel pennant adorned the wall over the grey slate mantelpiece.

"Hello Dad."

Joel Penfield did not rise to greet Henry. He flashed a toothy smile and pointed to a leather sofa, reserving the matching recliner for Malcolm. "Henry. Thanks for coming. Where is your girlfriend? Her name is Nancy, isn't it?

"Her name is Naomi and she is at her parent's home helping her mother prepare supper. Thanks for asking." He had alerted Joel twice that Naomi was not attending. The Alzheimers was worsening.

"The Packers Lions game is just starting. I like Brett Favre," said Henry.

"He's a great QB," said Joel.

"A real winner," said Henry.

Malcolm entered, wearing preppy chinos, a navy-blue crewneck sweater and low-cut walking shoes garnished by argyle socks. He sat in the recliner, propped up his feet and yawned. "Hello Dad and baby brother. Is dinner almost ready. I am famished."

"Hello Son," said Joel.

"Nice of you to join us," said Henry.

"Join you? I live here. It is you stopping by. You are the visitor. I am the resident."

"I would say boarder, but you pay no rent. Freeloader is apt," said Henry.

"How is the dissertation coming along?" asked Joel.

"Tough sledding, but I can handle it."

Henry leaned forward, feigning genuine interest. "What was the topic again? I forgot."

"It seems Dad's Alzheimers is contagious. Or is it hereditary?" said Malcolm.

Henry snapped his fingers. "I remember. You are writing on the earth-shaking topic of teenage love between teenagers Romeo and Juliet and the licentious affair of the Queen in Hamlet screwing her brother-in-law. Thrilling work."

Malcolm smiled condescendingly. "That is close even for a pedestrian mind like yours. The title of the thesis is illicit love among the royalty. Old

Will had a distinct distaste for infidelity."

"Too bad Shakespeare is not around to write about your hero, William Jefferson Clinton. Skank master in Chief. The title would be, Willy does the Intern."

Malcolm's lips pursed for a second before he spit out, "Screw you Mister Sanctimony."

Bernice called from the dining room. "Dinner! Come and get it."

Joel did not rise. "I want to watch football."

"Dad, it is Thanksgiving. Come join your family," said Henry.

"Leave the sound on, so I can hear it," said Joel.

"No way," said Joel, red-faced, agitated.

Henry stood by him as Malcolm headed to the dining room.

"Mother. You are a gem and you're grateful, starving oldest son thanks and praises you."

Henry guided Joel to the head of the table. His once strong father walked sheepishly ahead, like a child lost in the woods.

Bernice cooked like Julia Child on steroids. The sumptuous turkey meal, complete with mashed potatoes, gravy, asparagus, seemed to calm the air between the brothers. Dessert was homemade bread pudding and a pumpkin pie from Bredenbeck's bakery.

"Mom. That was an amazing meal. Thank you," said Henry.

She blew him a kiss. "My pleasure, my younger Son."

Malcolm rose and toasted her. "Mother you are as beautiful as Dante's beloved Beatrice. Saluda."

"Green Bay just went ahead," muttered Joel.

They exchanged glances. "He thanks you, Mom," said Henry.

"I have an announcement," said Malcolm.

"You finally lost your virginity," said Henry.

Malcolm laughed. "Close. My girlfriend Cheryl McMasters is with child. You will be grandparents in May. Hip, hip hooray."

Bernice gasped. "Dear sweet Lord."

"I hope it is a boy," said Joel. "Girls are a pain in the ass to raise."

Henry offered his hand. "Congratulations. I did not think you had it in you."

Malcolm ignored the outstretched hand.

"Perhaps you thought I was gay. Wrong! We are going to marry on Christmas Eve. It will be a very private affair. My best friend Jerome Harris will be best man and his wife Charlotte will be maid of honor," said Malcolm.

"They are black," said Joel.

"Grin and bear it Dad. We live in a diverse world," said Malcolm.

Malcolm stared at Henry. "Rome is like a brother to me."

"My brother is an only child," said Henry.

"Thanks to God, Joel will see his grandchild," said Bernice.

Henry looked at Joel as he inched away, his ears perked up to the football game.

God bless him and help him, thought Henry. And Mom too.

Bernice whispered. "I want to see you two in the library, now."

Bernice sat in a high-backed chair usually reserved for Joel, instantly surprising both sons. She looked queenly, austere, and yet loving.

"Sit there," she said pointing to a love seat. Henry complied, but Malcolm plopped into a side chair.

"I see you two cannot even sit beside each other. Well, I have news for both of you. After the holidays, I am committing your father to a Memory Care unit for his dementia. His dementia is now complicated by pancreatic cancer. He has six months to live."

Malcolm's jaw dropped. "OMG! That is horrible."

Henry dropped his face into his hands, rubbing his eyes as if to awake him from a bad dream.

"Six months? Mom, I am so sorry."

Bernice lifted her chin. "Do not shed any tears for me. Your father is a good husband and loved me ever since we laid eyes on each other. Thank God he might live to see a grandchild."

"Mom. What can I do?" said Henry.

"Nothing. There is nothing to do."

Malcolm rose and paced the room. "I was going to ask you and Dad if my family could move in."

"They may move in. Your father may find some comfort watching your wife's belly grow and knowing his legacy will carry on."

"Have you gotten a second opinion," asked Henry.

"Second and third. Both confirm the prognosis. Your father will be dead by Easter. Now go back in there and watch the football game with him. And no bickering or I shall take a broom to both of you."

The brothers walked away, not glancing at each other. Joel called out, "Way to go Packers!"

Bernice took Henry aside. "Henry, this family dynamic is sure to change. You will become the true man of the family. Someday you must show true leadership and reconcile with Malcolm. Promise me you will do so before I go to your father."

Henry's eyes filled up. He felt she had passed a weight and a blessing on him.

"Yes, Mother. I will do as you ask."

She took his hand in hers and patted it. "That's my boy."

William Shakespeare Penfield was born on the fifteenth of May. He would be an only child. Just like his father mused Henry. Malcolm's wife Cheryl was a Main liner. A graduate of Bryn Mawr College and the daughter of heart doctor Horace McMaster. Pretty and smart, she led Malcolm by the nose. She tried to take charge of the house, but Mother Bernice would not relinquish her crown to anyone.

Malcolm finished his dissertation three months later and started teaching as an Assistant Professor at Penn. He also developed a taste for single malt scotch. Not a day passed that he did not sip his Scotch in the Library.

Henry's construction company grew into the largest paving company in Southeastern Pennsylvania. Henry moved from the carriage house into a condo overlooking Rittenhouse Square in downtown Philly.

Over the next eighteen years, the brothers sparred at each family gathering much to the consternation of Bernice, now inflicted with multiple sclerosis.

Henry avoided marriage, settling for numerous flings with attractive women. He liked the status of eligible bachelor. Variety is the spice of life, someone said. Henry liked spicy women.

The night of the 2016 election found Malcolm tweeting his moral outrage. "Hillary was right. Trump's win is historical proof of the adage, the masses are the asses."

Henry tweeted back. "Kiss my deplorable ass."

By 2019, William was a sophomore at Penn. He studied computer science, not pursuing the liberal arts education his father cherished. Instead, he felt drawn to his successful Uncle Henry who gave him a part-time job running computerized estimates for paving contracts. William liked the mathematical certainty of the computer more than the ambiguity of existential philosophy or the intricate poetry of T.S. Eliot or the subtlety of the poetry of Ezra Pound or the raging verses of Alan Ginsberg.

Bernice summoned Henry to meet her on a day no one was home.

They sat in the library. Bernice had grown pale and barely left her wheelchair.

"Henry, I know you have tried, but God's clock runs faster as one ages. You must, We must save Malcolm from drink and bring the family together. Have you got a plan?"

"No."

She clasped his wrist, digging her nails into his suit jacket. "I have scarce time left."

Henry sighed aloud. "I will do what I have to do, what you want me to do."

"Then as Shakespeare said, if it were done when it be done well it be done quickly."

"As you wish. Who said that line? Juliet?"

"Dear God, no! Lady Macbeth."

"She too was a queen."

"An evil one."

On July Fourth night, William Penfield left home in an Uber X to attend the fireworks Celebrate America party along the Ben Franklin Parkway in front of the Art Museum. The Rocky statue stood at the base of the seventy-two steps leading up to the point where Rocky leaped, in anticipated triumph, his muscular arms held high before his match with

Apollo Creed for the heavyweight championship. To entertain the crowd, the City lined up Jennifer Hudson, The Philly Pops, and the U.S. Army field band. The festivities would end at midnight with a spectacular firework show,

At two am, Malcolm received a call from William's cell phone. "We have your punk ass son. If you do not pay us one million dollars in forty-eight hours, we will cut him into little pieces and feed him to the fish in the Delaware River. If you bring in the police or FBI, he will be killed immediately."

Shocked, Malcolm struggled to speak. "I do not have a million dollars."

The kidnapper laughed. "Get it from your brother or we start by making William a Wilhelmina."

The phone went dead.

Malcolm called Henry and told him what happened.

"Come to my house now," said Henry. "Do not tell your family anything."

Malcolm's stomach squeezed into a sailor's knot. "Yes, Henry."

Henry paced the floor of his living room while Malcolm retold the story of the call.

"They have his iPhone, correct?"

"Yes."

"Call them. Announce that I am listening, and the call is on speaker, but it is not being recorded. We are alone. No cops, as they demanded."

"What if they do not believe me?"

Henry grabbed Malcolm by the shirt collar. "This is not a debate. Do as I say for William's sake."

Embarrassed at having to follow Henry's lead, Malcom complied. The call was answered immediately.

"Do you have the money? Yes or no?" he asked in a nasally twang.

"This is Henry Penfield. Before we agree to any terms with you, we need proof of life. Take a photo of William and send it to my cell. 215 205 2379."

"Sure. He looks a little worse for the wear, but he is alive, at least for now."

Henry scribbled, "Kensington accent. White male. Probably under thirty."

The picture arrived, showing William with a black eye, swollen lips and a dazed look. Malcolm screamed. "What have you done to my son?"

"Just a little ass whipping. He looks better with a black eye."

Henry put a finger over Malcolm's lips. "Thank you for sending the photo. There is a problem with getting you the money. It is Friday morning of a four-day holiday. I need time to pull the full amount together. The best I can do is fifty grand now, the rest by Tuesday."

"Tuesday! That is bullshit. We want it all or Willy boy here loses pieces of his anatomy every hour on the hour starting at five PM tomorrow."

"Call me after nine thirty in the morning. I need time to go to my bank for a loan against my company. I guess you know I own a paving company."

"Yeah. We know all about you, Dude. Don't play us for chumps or Shakespeare here turns into a tragedy." The voice hung up.

Henry pointed to the kitchen. "Malcolm, go make coffee. I need to check my employee files. I may know who they are and where they are holding William."

"How could you know that? I need money not detective work."

"For once in your life, do as I say. You are not one iota smarter than me when it comes to the real world of Philly. I pave the streets, and nobody knows them better than me. I take my coffee with cream, no sugar."

"Yes. I remember. You always said you did not like anything that made you sweet. Sweetness was weakness was how you put it."

Henry pulled up his employee files and did a search on employees living in zip code 19125. Three names came up. Mary Porter, a secretary, age fifty-two. Nate Gant, a black truck driver. Maxwell Kelly, a laborer age twenty-nine living on Tulip Street. Bingo! Kelly was hired as a favor to his uncle, Councilman Jules Catrone. He had a criminal record for assault. Henry hired Max Kelly at Catrone's request. Henry needed a variance for a side road off Girard Avenue. Catrone got him the variance in exchange for hiring his nephew. The punk later beat a burglary charge thanks to his uncle.

Henry took the coffee cup, stirring it with a spoon. "I think I know where they are holding William. This kidnapping seems improvised. They recognized him and offered William a ride home from the celebration.

"They took him to a house on Tulip Street. We are going there now."

"Shouldn't we call the police?"

"You never know who Catrone has in his pocket. In Philly, there are two degrees of separation. Everybody knows everybody."

Henry pressed a brick on his fireplace. The brick slid aside and opened a small compartment. Henry extracted a nine-millimeter Glock with no serial number.

"What the hell? You are bringing a gun?" asked Malcolm.

"We are going to the drug capital of the City. I am not bringing a knife to a gun fight. If you want to stay here, please do so. If not, just stay out of my way. You got that older brother?"

Malcolm blanched. "Yeah. I am scared."

"Me too."

Henry drove past the target house, a rundown, semi-detached frame home. A light was on in the living room. The low windows just above the ground no doubt opened into a basement. Henry parked the car and took a flashlight from the glove compartment. Crouching, they walked around the house to the rear yard. They crept low along the side of the house. Henry forced open a window to the basement. His flashlight scoured the basement. William lay on a sofa, his hands tied, a gag around his mouth. He was alone.

Henry gave Malcolm a thumbs up. He whispered, "We are going in and out of this window. You go in first and untie Will. I will cover you from here. Be very quiet and he will be on his way home in five minutes."

Malcolm nodded, "Got it."

He climbed through the narrow window, slid down the basement wall, landing feet first. Will awoke, staring wide-eyed at the spectacle of his father climbing into the basement. Malcolm held a finger to his lips. He untied Will and they raced to the open window; Malcom shoved William's butt to push him above ground.

Malcolm climbed into the opening when a voice behind yelled, "What the hell?"

It was the same voice from the phone call.

"Stop!" said the voice.

Henry yanked Malcolm to safety. Max Kelly fired at Henry. The bullet struck his left shoulder. Henry yelped in pain, dropping his gun near Malcolm. Malcolm grabbed the gun, his hand shaking.

"Shoot him," said Henry.

Malcolm quivered. He closed his eyes and fired two shots at Kelly. He missed. Max retreated up the stairs. Malcolm handed his iPhone to Will.

"Call 911. Now."

Malcolm dragged Henry towards the car. Kelly emerged at the corner; his gun pointed at them.

"Stop!" screamed Kelly.

Malcolm fired a third shot, catching Kelly in his right hip. The impact sent Kelly backwards until he fell in a heap.

"Leave Max. We gotta boogie like we were never here," said another man.

"We can't just leave him," said a second voice.

"He ain't family. Let's go," said the first voice.

Police sirens seared the night air. Malcolm put away the Glock. He knelt by Henry. "Hang in Brother. You saved Will. I owe you."

"I will send you a bill."

The police arrived; their guns drawn. "What happened here?" asked a black patrolman.

Malcolm rose. "My brother was shot. We need a doctor."

"Who are you?"

"I am Professor Malcolm Penfield. I work at Penn. This is my son William who was abducted by three men. They were holding him at this house. My brother Henry and I pulled him out of the house. Please get a medical team here to help my brother. The man lying over there is Max Kelly. I shot him with my brother's gun."

"Where is the gun?"

"In my pocket. Please retrieve it. My hands are shaking."

The policeman recovered the gun. "We will need a statement from all three of you. You took down Max Kelly. Imagine Max being stoned by a college professor."

Malcom thrust back his shoulders and held his head high, like soldiers on parade. "We are Penfields, Officer. We stick together. Nobody screws with our family."

"Officer. Make sure this little incident does not go public. My brother is a Professor at Penn and bad publicity is not good news," said Henry.

"Count on it," said the Officer.

Henry reached out his hand to Malcolm. They clasped hands. William knelt beside Henry.

"Thank you, Uncle Henry."

Malcolm knelt beside his son and brother, embracing both. "Son, remember this day when we truly became a family."

"Yes, Dad."

Malcolm smiled. "After all, this is the City of Brotherly love."

Henry nodded.

Late that night, Henry dialed Bernice from his car parked along East River Drive near the Art Museum.

"Mission Impossible completed," he said.

"Thanks be to God."

"When you see Dad, please tell him our secret."

"He will be proud," she said.

"Good night Mom."

"Good night sweet Prince."

"Hamlet?"

"Yes!"

Ten minutes later, a Cadillac Escalade pulled up beside his car. The driver lowered the window.

"Hello Henry," said Jules Catrone.

Henry handed Jules an envelope. "Thanks Jules. The envelope is for Max and our police friends and a little something for you. The boys did a good job pretending the blanks were real."

"Drama runs in the family. That shiner we gave him was a little memento."

"He'll never forget it. He can tell his grandkids fifty years from now."

Jules saluted Henry. “Nice doing business with ya.”

"Ditto."

Henry drove away towards Independence Hall. He passed the Hall, stopping for a second to offer the Hall a thumbs up.

“God bless America.”

The White Tiger

Exhausted after ten hours of caring for Corona virus patients at Chestnut Hill Hospital, Doctor Robert Dylan Hart longed for a Mary Jane and a nap. He had given up the evil weed smoking habit on his thirtieth birthday, four years ago for his health. The irony that he was caring for Covid 19 patients and susceptible to catching the virus suggested that life has no rules, no safe places, no plan. Marijuana was medicinal, self-prescribed.

He took the elevator to the top floor then used the fire escape to reach the door to the roof where he could puff away in privacy. The chilly late October air greeted him with a hard slap.

The Hill was the highest point in Philly, leading him closer to heaven. A mist shrouded the Hill like a mantle. The virus ran rampant, embedded in the heavy air, a deadly, cloud casting a pall over all of Philly.

The air seemed to grasp the City's throat in a vise, just like the virus that closed the City down.

He lit up a joint savoring the easeful warmth. "God bless cannabis," he whispered to the night sky.

The fire door opened to nurse Maribeth Lucci. He was happy to see her angelic face. Short and slightly overweight, her full breasts bulged under her white safety gown. A tiny gold crucifix hung from her neck.

"Here's company. Care for a toke?" he asked, smiling.

Maribeth strode toward him, her soft brown eyes peeping from red lined sockets.

"I thought you'd be here. Yes. I will take a hit. Lord knows I need it."

They stood together at the edge of the roof, staring at the full moon.

"Here it is Halloween, and we are blessed with a blue moon. Ghosts and goblins abound below seeking candy. What a wondrous world we live in," he said wistfully.

"There are few kids out trick or treating. The virus has chased them inside."

"True. I stopped by to see Clarence Mayes earlier. He insists there is a white tiger hell bent on devouring him. We should consider changing his Meds," said Maribeth.

"Duly noted. If his lungs were working, I would give the old dude a hit."

"I bet he would appreciate it. The man has seen the world."

"I hope so. The virus is getting worse and the promise of a vaccine seems to have the world marching to a distant drummer."

Maribeth snuggled next to his six-foot-three frame, as if he was a prop to hold her upright. His strong torso felt like a wall.

"The scientists will find a cure."

"Yes, Maribeth. They will in time, until the next pandemic swoops out of China or Africa or Europe or even here and attacks mankind."

She tapped his flat belly. "Why so pessimistic?"

"Realistic. Humanity has seen any number of plagues going back centuries. It is like science cures one plague and another more sinister one sneaks out of the shadows to infest us. We are doomed to suffer them."

"What choice do we have other than to survive?"

Robert took a long pull on his joint. Inhaling the smoke deep into his lungs. He closed his eyes.

"None. We shall survive."

She pulled him close to her. "You better survive. I demand you survive."

"Bossy aren't you?"

She pulled his face to hers. "You need mothering."

"God forbid I have to suffer the strangulation from apron strings of a second mother. I must tend to Clarence."

His remark about motherhood pin pricked her heart.

"Go ahead. I need a moment to myself," she said, while running her fingertips over the crucifix.

He descended to the rooms below. What was troubling Maribeth?

First stop would be Clarence Mayes.

Robert entered the patient room of Clarence Mayes, a seventy-seven-year-old grandfather whose lithe body, infected by the virus, sweated like a day laborer picking fruit in the August sun. Clarence had been his patient for over a week. The virus had smothered Clarence's breathing. Yet he gasped and strained to stay alive like a drowning man in a wide lake, paddling for survival.

"How are you, Clarence?" asked Robert.

Clarence forced a nod under his respirator.

"I am still here, ain't I."

"That you are."

"Hey Doc. It's Halloween ain't it?"

"True that."

"I heard the nurses talking that there is a full, blue moon tonight. Do you believe full moons make women horny?"

The Doctor smiled, perpetually amazed at man's incomprehensible hunger for sex.

"That is a medical fact."

"Really? No shit! My ex-wife said I had a disease. She called it terminal screwinitis."

Robert tapped Clarence's forehead with a thermometer. The number read 103."

"Well, your passions may be as hot as your body. You are still a very sick man."

Clarence waved a forefinger. "I am going to beat this thing. I ain't ready to die. When I get out of here, maybe you can prescribe me some blue pills."

"Sure. Why not?"

The door swung open for Maribeth. She nodded to Robert.

"Doctor, I must take Mister Mayes' temperature."

"I just took it. He's burning at 103.6"

Maribeth flashed her soft brown eyes disapprovingly at him, nodded and took Clarence's temperature.

She checked his pulse reading on the bedside monitor.

"Yes. 103 it is. There will be no trick and treating for you tonight, Clarence."

"Seeing you pretty lady is my treat."

Maribeth exchanged a quick glance with Robert.

"No more thoughts of women. Save your strength for fighting the virus. Women should be your last priority. Keep them in your dreams," said Maribeth.

Clarence coughed, his chest shaking.

"Don't talk about dreams. I had a weird one last night, I dreamt a white tiger was after me. I was a kid fishing along the Wissahickon Creek in Fairmount Park near the old, covered bridge. I used to call it the Wissy. Pissy in the Wissy! Anyway, I had to pee, so I went into the woods and came face to face with this weird looking tiger. The beast was cross-eyed like my sister-in-law, Dottie. Well, I pissed my pants and ran out of there like I was running for my life. That darn tiger chased me, hissing hot breath on my butt. I thought I was going to be his dinner. Then it roared. I woke up. Weird stuff ain't it?"

Robert put up his hands in reassurance. "No. High fever often induces visions. The heated brain cells jumble up hallucinations."

"So, I ain't crazy?"

"No, Clarence. You are a man stuck in a crazy world plagued by a hideous disease."

"Thank god."

Robert smiled at the irony.

Maribeth pursed her lips. "I will say a Hail Mary for you."

"I need prayers. Lots of them."

"Don't we all," said Maribeth.

The emergency alarm blared, announcing the arrival of a new patient, sending Robert and Maribeth rushing out of Clarence's room.

"Go get 'em," said Clarence.

The moon rose in the night, high over the tall trees. Chestnut Hill is the highest point in Philly. The neighborhood closest to heaven. His fever rose, too. Sweat poured down his neck. Beads of warm perspiration soaked his gown at the shoulders. His legs shook uncontrollably. Nausea racked his stomach. He wanted water. Lots of water. Cold water. Soothing water. A cold shower. A winter storm of ice and snow.

But no relief came. He felt alone, tired, sick; pain was his only companion.

"You are dying Clarence," said a voice from his numbed mind.

White and blue gowned bodies raced back and forth in the corridor outside his room. "Where are they going? Who are they? Where am I? Who am I?" he asked to no one.

His chest heaved in desperation. He was drowning in a bed of incessant pain.

Then he saw the tiger. The beast moved across the room, stealthily, silent. A low growl followed a sinister hiss from foot long fangs. Clarence tried to remove his mask, but it was fastened to the heavy ventilator. He was trapped like a lamb with a broken leg.

His instinct was to fight, to protect himself. But he was defenseless, unable to run or fight. He clenched his fists, defiant though fearful to his toes.

The tiger stalked him under the overhead lights, like it was circling a campfire. Clarence's heart sank in resignation to his fate.

"I will fight you," he yelled, his nervous shout muffled by the mask.

Two shadows entered the room. A man and a woman.

The tiger vanished like smoke whisked away by a surging wind.

He exhaled, relieved that he had survived.

Maribeth checked his pulse. "His pulse rate is through the roof. She pressed a thermometer to his forehead. "One-o-three."

Robert stood over him. "Clarence. What caused you to scream?"

Clarence's chest heaved, then slowly sank as his body settled into an uneasy rest. "The tiger. It was ready to eat me like a cheesesteak. I think I did a pissy in the Wissie and that was his watering hole. Pissed him off, I did for sure."

"I'll change you," said Maribeth.

"No. I can do it myself," said Clarence.

Maribeth reached under his gown and snatched away the soggy depends. She took a clean one from the pile on the dresser and inserted it over his genitals.

"Thanks. You are a blessing," he said.

Robert sat on the edge of the bed. "You realize the tiger is not real don't you?"

"It's real to me."

"What do you think when you see it? Do you think God sent it here to punish you?"

"I have no idea what you mean."

Maribeth took Robert by the arm. "He needs to sleep. No more questions tonight."

Robert firmly took her hand from his arm. "Nurse, please do not interrupt my examination of my patient. I want to learn what he is feeling while it is fresh in his mind. Clarence, are you afraid of dying?"

"Isn't everybody? We all fear this Covid shit is gonna kill us all."

"History has seen worse plagues. We will survive this plague and all the ones that follow," explained Robert.

Clarence gasped. "Doc. Are you saying this Covid is gonna return? What about the vaccines the big shots say are gonna stop it?"

"We will persevere, but it is not the final battle mankind will fight for our survival."

"I don't get it. What you are saying is absurd," said Clarence.

"Yes. It is absurd. We cannot win. But we can fight. It is our fighting that keeps mankind alive."

"Hah! We are the damned underdogs. Just like the 2017 Eagles. They won the Super Bowl."

"And not much since," said Robert.

Maribeth put her hand to her mouth, in horror, as if hit by a bolt of truth.

"You are saying we are all doomed?"

"Eventually, we are all fighting a virus that is eternal, inhuman, and lethal."

"Do you believe in God and salvation?"

Robert clasped his hands on her shoulders.

"I believe we must fight on even if the fight is rigged. That is courage."

Maribeth edged away from Robert as if she were backing away from a dangerous animal.

"You! You, your Godless views. You are the white tiger, the faithless."

Robert laughed out loud, a cackling, nervous laugh, an ironic devilish laugh.

"Don't be absurd."

Maribeth positioned herself between Clarence and Robert.

"Get out of the room, now. Out!" she said.

"No. I am his doctor. I am going to save his life."

"Why? If it all means nothing to live, then why save a life?"

Robert turned his palms up, as if entreating mercy.

"It is what I do. It is what you do too. Is it not? We all die eventually. So, we must fight every day. Otherwise, living means nothing."

Maribeth recoiled, her eyes blank with fright. "I am not sure what either of us do nor why we are here."

Robert started to walk away. "Let's get back to work, nurse. We have a plague to fight. And a tiger to tame."

Maribeth made the sign of the cross. She whispered to the room.

"Our Father who art in heaven ..."

Election night on Tuesday brought Philly to an elevated state of tension. Police were dispatched in case of rioting, looting, or worse. The continuing rise of Covid cases intensified the aura of fear and edginess. The populace had suffered the mental duress of lost jobs, lost income, lack of freedom, and the fear of getting Covid.

Maribeth had voted by mail for Biden, though she was pro-life. No one could force her to abort the child in her womb. Not even Robert. She planned to tell him he was about to become a father in May. Hopefully, the child would be born into a Covid free world. She expected him to arrive around eight after his shift at Einstein. She made her rounds, checking temperatures, pulses, and medications.

All patients were quiet, too worried about whether they could breathe than who was winning the contentious election. Politics shrinks when one's life is in God's hands.

Robert was right. Prayers soothe soul, but the body needs medicine.The Country needed a vaccine.

She feared Robert would want an abortion. She would never agree to it unless there were mitigating medical issues. If needed, she would raise the child on her own.

At ten of eight Robert entered the ward and headed to the stairway. "I hope you have a joint with you," she whispered to his back.

He walked slowly, his head own, shoulders bent. He struggled to open the heavy door.

Maribeth waited three minutes before following him. The second she opened the door to the roof, she heard his loud, chest deep cough. She found his leaning against the inner wall.

"Rob. Are you alright?"

He coughed again, spitting out a baseball of phlegm. His face white, his eyes drooping, he forced a smile.

"I need a nurse. Know a good one?"

She texted her nurse partner. "Come to the roof stairwell. Bring orderlies. Stat."

Her news would have to wait.

Robert lay in a nervous sweat in the dimly lit room across the hall from Clarence. His head spun in a dizzying pain, like a hangover from drinking bad gin. The respirator belt and plastic mask reminded him of a Halloween mask he once wore. Was he dressed up as Batman or Spiderman that year?

"I am more like nowhere man," he thought.

A loud, familiar scream came from across the hall. Clarence.

The tiger must be on the prowl. How did I get to be prey?

Maribeth entered. She checked his vital signs. He felt embarrassed that she was now his caretaker, his superior.

She stroked his hair with her hand in a plastic glove. His mother always stroked his head. The Cancer Tiger had devoured her six years ago.

"You are a very sick man, Robert Dylan Hart."

"Am I knocking on heaven's door?"

"No Bobby D. You are tapping on the devil's front door."

"That's not funny. I heard Clarence whooping it up. Is he chasing the devil too or is it chasing him? How long have I been out of it?"

"About eighteen hours."

"Doctors are not supposed to get sick. We have office hours and do not make appointments for ourselves. Have you slept at all?"

"A little. I showered in the locker area this morning and slept there on a cot. Thanks for asking."

"You are welcome."

"Shall I call down for a meal for you?"

"No. I am too tired to eat. What is going on with the world? How many new cases have been reported?"

Maribeth squeezed his hand. "I do not know, and you do not need to know. Leave it to others to save the world."

"It all seems so damned futile." He closed his eyes as tears welled at the edges of each eye.

"There is always hope."

"Struggle yes. Hope is a dream, a fantasy. Banking on hope is like betting against a pat hand in poker. Is this institution late on paying its water bill?"

"I will get you some," she said.

"It's a mad, mad world."

Clarence tossed and turned struggling to sleep, gasping for air. His brain seared by fear, he sat up, looking for Maribeth. A nurse dressed in white stood silhouetted in the doorway to his room. Fearful, he laid down, pulling the sheet over his mask, hiding from the white image.

The white figure turned away. Clarence ripped off his mask. He headed to the hallway, finding it empty. The door to Robert's room was ajar. Clarence slipped into the room. A masked white figure lay asleep, its chest heaving, so now was his chance to slay the beast.

He unhooked the floor lamp and charged the sleeping beast, striking it in the head. The beast howled. He struck it again and again and again until he was spent. He dropped the bloody lamp on the floor and staggered toward his room.

Maribeth saw him leave Robert's room, his gown red with fresh blood.

"Dear God. God. God!" she screamed.

She raced past Clarence and found Rob, her lover, father of her child lying in a pool of blood. Unconscious.

He had a pulse. She quickly sent a Stat message to hospital staff. She gathered towels and pillowcases and began pressing on the wounds to stem the rush of blood. She pressed the call for emergency staff on her iPhone.

"You must live Rob. You must live."

The clatter of footsteps signaled the arrival of six staffers.

"I need nurses here. You orderlies subdue and restrain patient Mayes. Call the police. We have a madman on our hands. He tried to kill Doctor Hart. Move!"

They wheeled Robert on a gurney to the ER. Her hands and uniform bloody, Maribeth stayed at Robert's side. Tears slid down her cheeks. Clutching her crucifix, she asked to no one.

"Why? Dear God. Why?"

As the orderlies dragged Clarence away, he yelled, "I did it, Nurse. I saved the world. The tiger is dead! I can pissie in the Wissie!"

Three weeks later, on Thanksgiving morning, Maribeth finished her shift at six AM. On the two-hundred-yard walk to Mother of Consolation Roman Catholic Church, she managed to say half of the rosary. She entered through a side door, walked to the votive candles, and lit two. One for Robert. One for Clarence. This is the Church I was christened in. Here Father Conklin heard my first confession. Here is where I would have been married. Here is where my child will be baptized.

The marble walls and statues cast a stony, uncaring pallor. The stained-glass windows sparkled with images she could not fathom. She felt like a stranger in a strange land.

She wanted to pray, but the only person who she could pray for was inside her.

"Where are you my Lord?" she called out.

Robert and Clarence had both died on the twenty-third of November. Their deaths were listed in the newspaper as Covid 19 related.

Cold, untruthful statistics. Numbers on a chart. Would she die as a number? Would some distant viruses infect and kill her child?

She felt contaminated.

She realized that to be human is to be condemned to fight eternally. She would live for and through her child. The child would perpetuate her soul.

To be human is not to endlessly despair. It is to live and fight, to find salvation through her life on earth. She would name her child after its father. God willing, she would marry and bear more soldiers for the human army.

She finished the rosary and left thinking of enjoying this first Thanksgiving with her child. A cool wind hastened her to her duties. A nurse's work is never done.

Later, she climbed the steps to the roof. She looked over the grey city. The City was sick. Businesses were closed. People were huddled inside homes they may lose. Though Philly always comes back from a loss. Toughness and tenacity is the City's DNA. The old saying on the Street was "You never lose a fight if you do not quit."

Round two starts today.

"Round two! Yes, "The Eye of the Tiger!""

Then, like an epiphany, a song loved by Philly seared her mind with newfound strength. The uplifting soundtrack from *Rocky Three* stirred her blood. Philly people do not quit.

Like the tiger, they rise up. Undaunted. Unafraid. Unconquerable.

The End.

Want to Read More?

Meet Ro Ro Morse, a sexy and wavy Philadelphia Police Detective with a brain for justice and a heart for bad boys. Will Ro Ro escape the dangerous, seductive relationship with the notorious criminal Germantown John and bring him to justice or will she give everything up for love? Find out with two free chapters from Ro Ro Morse Philadelphia's Most Fearsome Detective:

https://bit.ly/roromorsefreestory

www.ingramcontent.com/pod-product-compliance
Lightning Source LLC
Chambersburg PA
CBHW070403200726
48294CB00003B/1065

* 9 7 8 1 7 3 4 5 7 1 9 8 1 *